The Book of Barry

Sage Advice for Life, Love, and Business

Barry McLeod

Recommendations

Barry did more than just believe in me. He taught me to believe in myself. And that is all I ever needed. *Kelli LaPorte*

Barry shares his knowledge very willingly with others and in an easy to understand straightforward way. Through his efforts and teaching, he has helped me get past some road blocks and out of my comfort zone to achieve more than I thought I could. I am proud to call him friend. *Jeanette MacFarlane*

Barry to me was a mentor, a teacher, a best friend and was like another dad. He taught me life lessons I can use for the rest of my life. *Kyle Thomas*

Having Mr. McLeod as a mentor was like having a dad; he knew all the right things to say .... With every situation I encountered, he had an experience and I was able to learn how to make the right decisions based on his experience. The Book of Barry was like a daily devotional, there was always something new to be said that took my breath away. *Brittany Browning*

Barry's teachings have truly changed my life for the better and not only me but the people around me as well. I'm tremendously grateful to call him my good friend and cannot wait to learn more from him as the years go on. Just like he says to me, I say back to him: "Mr. McLeod, you're stuck with me for life." *Kayla DeLaMora*

The experience I had as Barry's mentee can be explained in one word: Energy! Barry always has it and always talks about it. He tells me all the time that if I put good energy into the world I will always get good energy back. Three years after the first time I have heard that it still cannot be more true. *Mackenzie Lewis*

I have been working and doing training calls with Barry for over three years. I continue to learn and grow from his expertise in networking. Barry has been a loyal, trusted, good friend and is someone that I have learned to depend on. He truly cares for the people that he works with. *Richard Johnson*

The only word that comes to mind when I hear the name "Barry McLeod" is the word ineffable. To have someone that believes in you and sees the amazing things that I didn't see in myself. He strives to make me see the best

version of myself and that has to be the best feeling in the world.
Travis Alvarez

Barry McLeod has been an extremely helpful mentor. He has been more than a helping hand, he is an iron bar holding me up. His wise wisdom always helps me when I am struggling with adversity. He has impacted my life for the better. He has changed the way I live. My life has never been more positive and happy since meeting him.
Phillip Freedman

Barry McLeod is one of the most inspiring and enthusiastic motivational trainers that I have ever listened to. His desire to help people achieve their goals and dreams is contagious. Barry lives by, practices, and teaches the true meaning of team work! *Brenda Johnson*

We all have disappointments in life but Barry's positive words of encouragement always help lift me up and give me the strength to go on. *Ginger Blalock*

Barry McLeod is undeniably the best at telling a story and weaving it into an action plan for success, not just in business but in all aspects of life. His years of coaching and mentoring youth and his networking team has inspired people to rise to levels they didn't believe were possible. Everyone needs a copy of "The Book of Barry" and get extras to share with everyone you care about. *Jacki Smith*

Dedication

I dedicate this book to my family:

My wife, Cindy McLeod

My children and grandchildren

>   Tracy McLeod
>
>   Troy, Jill, Sarah, and Conner McLeod
>
>   Tangie, Randy, Kyle, Dylan, and Dustin Chavez
>
>   Travis, Nicole, Gunner, Chiales, and Asher McLeod
>
>   Anthony, Shelly, Keagan, and Mac McLeod
>
>   Amber McLeod
>
>   Audrey McLeod
>
>   Jared, Jolene, Logan, and Easton Bradley

My parents, brothers, sisters, and cousins

>   Harold and Audrey McLeod
>
>   Paul and Guy Cottino and Family
>
>   Lori, Tim, and Caleb LeMaster
>
>   Becky and Steve Beisinger and Family
>
>   Roger Neukam and Family

Arnie and Jean Nelson

Rev. David Nelson and Family

Daniel Nelson and Family

Dave and Elaine Braucher

The Walker Family

Contents

Preface

Before you begin, I want you to know that in this book there is a hidden meaning just for you. I promise that each person reading this book may find something different— something especially for you. H.B. Brooks, the great hockey coach from the story, *Miracle on Ice*, said, "You were born for this … this is your time, now go out there and take it."

One of my favorite lines from the movie "Field of Dreams" says, "There comes a time when all the cosmic tumblers have clicked into place and the universe opens itself up for only a moment to show you what is possible." It's time for you! May that be the case for each of you as you absorb the messages on these pages and as you relate to these stories. Throughout this book you will find extraordinary stories of everyday people, people that I know personally. These individuals have made a difference in their own lives as they help others make a difference in theirs. Why not you and why not now? Take massive and immediate action. Dream big dreams. Remember that all things are possible to those who believe.

Introduction

You may say I'm a dreamer …

This book that you are holding in your hands has been a long time in the making. For years, I've given business seminars, mentored students, and taught Sunday school classes. When I share with my audiences the lessons I've learned, I always say, "This is out of the Book of Barry, so take it for what it's worth." Some of the high school students I've mentored finally started to pester me, asking, "Well, where is this 'Book of Barry'?"

My wife Cindy and I talked about it, and we realized that the time had come to make *The Book of Barry* a reality. Why? My goal for this book is a simple one: to add hope and value to people's lives.

How do I intend to do that? What I want to share in this book are lessons I've learned, principles I've come to understand, and practical tools that you can use to make changes in your life.

When I'm giving seminars, I tell people that I'm not the big guru at the top of the mountain. I've probably had more failures than everyone in the room combined. But I didn't let those failures keep me down. I kept getting up. I kept moving forward. I knew what I wanted in life, and I learned how to make the changes I needed to make to live the life that I wanted to live.

I believe that success always leaves clues, just as failure does. I've had plenty of both—in sports, in business, and in my life—and the clues I've taken from each of those successes and failures have all become part of *The Book of Barry*. It's not theory; I only teach principles that I know have already been time-tested and field-tested throughout my life.

It all started when I was just a young kid. I was painfully thin and so I was always embarrassed to take my shirt off in PE class. I wasn't a very good athlete, so when they would choose up sides for different teams—whether it be softball, kickball, or any other sport—I was always one of the last to be picked. It was embarrassing. One of my most painful moments came at an early age. I was on a basketball team, but I wasn't very good, which meant that I mostly stayed on the bench. One day my mom and dad came to watch our game. It was a bad day, and we were losing big time. But even though we were getting beat by thirty points, the coach waited until the last minute—literally, the last sixty seconds of the game—to put me in. I was horribly embarrassed about that.

I made two decisions that day. The first was that I would never let such a thing happen to me again. I became determined to make myself a better ball player, and I did. The second decision was that if I ever had the opportunity to coach a ball team, I would never do that to anyone else. I would never put anyone in such an embarrassing situation. In later years I had the opportunity to coach many ball teams, and I never did that to kids. My players knew that if they got into a ball game, it was because they had earned it. How did they earn it? They came to practice, they worked hard, and they improved themselves. No one on Barry McLeod's teams was ever put into a game out of pity. It was always because they had earned it, and the kids appreciated it. They knew when they went into a game that they could hold their heads high; they deserved to be there.

As a coach, I had plenty of successes. I took kids that nobody wanted and created a dynasty with them. We won championships five years in a row.

In business, I've had lots of failures, but I've also had very good successes. I'm no one's guru. I'm a person just like you, who has been able to make a success in my own world that I would love to share with others who need some hope in their lives.

We all have choices. We can either accept the negatives in our lives or we can do something about them. Throughout my life I've been a fighter and I've been a crusader. I've always cheered for the underdog, and I've found so many times in life that underdogs can win if they believe they can.

I've learned a lot of lessons like that. I'm no different from you or from anyone else. I've walked in your shoes. I understand where you're coming from, and in this book I want to show you how I've used some of those lessons to make myself a better person. I want you to know that you can do that too.

There was a time in my life when I was in a serious financial mess. I didn't know what to do. I walked into the bathroom, looked myself in the mirror, and said, "Yes, you're in a mess. And this mess is your own fault. You created it with your negative thinking. But you can uncreate it with better thinking." And from that day on, I've been a maniac on a mission—a mission not only to improve myself, but also to help the people around me, people who wanted to do better than they had done, or to be better than they had been.

An important part of my mission has been to help put hope back into people's lives and to help them start dreaming again. I've learned from my own life that all dreams are possible if you believe. It's time to start believing again. It's time to start dreaming again. Remember those dreams you had, maybe years ago? Let's take them out of the closet, and dust them off, and make them a reality.

I truly believe that if you study this book, you will find some golden nugget here that speaks to you. I don't know if you're going to find it in the first part of the book, or the last part of the book, or somewhere in between, but I promise each of my readers that there's a message in here that is specifically designated just for you. It will be different for each individual reader, but it will be there. You just need to find your message and then, once you've found it, take action and put it to work.

Someone once said that all study is fruitless unless you make changes with it and put it into action. So I encourage you, as you read this book, to find that message that's just for you. Find your golden nugget, and then apply it, and strengthen it, and use it. You can make your dreams come true and you can make the world a better place for everyone.

1. What's on Your Window?

The stories in your mind
become the stories of your life.
Kody Bateman

Imagine yourself living in a beautiful beach house, with huge windows overlooking the ocean. The view is crystal clear and perfect. You can see the beach, the waves, maybe even a gorgeous sunrise or sunset. Over time, the windows become clouded and grimy. Unless you do something to keep those windows clean, your once-beautiful view becomes distorted.

Guess what? The same thing happens in your own mind.

The computer in your head

Understand that the human brain is the most massive and complex computer that exists. Throughout our lives, every experience, every sensation, every thought, every feeling comes into that computer—into our thought processes and subconscious mind—and they stay there. We absorb them all. Like a computer, the subconscious mind takes in all the information given to it. It acts on the information it receives; it doesn't know any difference between what's true and what's false or what's good and what's bad. But unlike the computer, the mind has no delete button.

All of our thoughts, statements and experiences—both true and false—come together to shape our beliefs. We take those beliefs and use them to form what I call the **belief window**. That belief window becomes a filtering system for everything that we do. We start collecting beliefs and putting them on that belief window. Pretty soon that once-clear window is clouded with all the things that we have put on it.

And all too often, what we put on our belief window is negative junk. Think about it. It's negative messages like: "You're not a good ball player ... you're overweight ... you're dumb ... you're too thin ... you can't pass the test ... you can't graduate from school ... you'll never find love ... you can never get that job ... you'll never have a successful relationship." Any of those sound familiar? I'll bet they do, and I'm sure you can add more.

Looking at your life through that window that you've created in your own mind is just like being inside your house looking out your window at the view. Everything that you see through that window is colored by what you have put on the window.

Let me give you an example. As I mentioned in the introduction, when I was a little kid, I was painfully thin. I was not a good athlete. So what did I put on my belief window back then? "Wow, I'm embarrassed to take my shirt off. I'm embarrassed to be so thin that people make comments about how thin I am." "Wow, I get picked last for the team. I'm not a very good athlete. I hate it when we go to PE because I know what's going to happen and kids laugh at me."

All of these experiences—whatever they may be—get put on your belief window. If we don't do anything about them, then we carry those beliefs all the way through our lives. Those beliefs come to determine who we are and who we are not, what we can do and what we can't do. As in our computer analogy, you can think of the belief window as your programming or your operating system. It controls your actions—and your results.

It would be hard to overstate how powerful that belief window can be. Let me tell you a story. It's one of my favorite examples of the power of the belief window.

The power of the belief window

You'll remember that I told you I wasn't a very good athlete when I was young. I worked to overcome that and make myself a better player, and years later, I was privileged to play in a basketball championship game.

It wasn't looking good for our team. We were literally 11 points behind with 55 seconds to play. By every indication, the game was over. This was back in the days before the three-point shot, so you had to pick up two points at a time. The other team had just made a free throw to put them up by 11. Our coach called a time out; we came back to our bench and they went to theirs. Our coach said, "Look over there." They were all going crazy. They were high-fiving each other. In the stands, their fans were all hugging each other. It was a tremendous outpouring of celebration.

Our coach said to us, "This is totally unacceptable. We are not going to let this happen. When they go back out there to shoot this other foul shot, they're going to miss it. We're going to rebound it and go down the floor."

There was a player on the other team that I had known for years. We always ended up guarding each other. When we walked back onto the court, he was standing right next to me. As they were getting ready to take the foul shot, he leaned over and whispered into my ear, "Barry, I can't believe we finally beat you guys in a championship game." I replied, "I don't believe it."

What was on our belief windows at that moment? The other team was having a hard time believing they were going to beat us, even though the odds against us were astronomical. Thanks to our coach, our team didn't believe that they would beat us. We believed—we knew—that we were going to pull it out. Some way, somehow, we would pull it out. Remember, we not only had to score ten points to get close, we also had to stop them from scoring. There was no shot clock back then, so we had to stop them from dribbling out the clock. We had to steal the ball and pressure them into making mistakes.

As those last 55 seconds ticked down, we narrowed their lead to four points. There was another time out called and our coach said, "Now look." We looked down at their side and their fans weren't hugging each other anymore. They were standing there in silence. Their players weren't high-fiving each other anymore. They were pointing fingers and blaming each other. Sure enough, with three or four seconds left on the clock, we had the ball one point down. We had scored ten points.

Our best player on the team got the ball, but they had him surrounded. Luckily for me, he got a bullet pass to me at the top of the key and I shot it. As I went up to shoot, that kid who had guarded me for years actually came flying through to block the shot. He knocked me down and we both fell to the floor watching the ball go through the air. It was one of those Kodak moments. The referee didn't blow the whistle; he wasn't going to call a foul on the last play of the championship game. The ball went through the net, and it was all over.

We had won the championship, just as our collective belief window told us we would. The other team didn't really believe that they could win, and they didn't.

For several years after that tremendous win, people would always say, "Barry, how did it feel to make that last shot?" I always said, "Hey, ask the other five guys who made those five baskets to get us to that point." If they hadn't have done that, my shot would have been meaningless. Of course it was a great moment for me, as the kid who had always been the last to be picked for any team. But what mattered most was that I—along with the rest of our team—had learned to believe that we could win.

Do you know what's on your belief window? There's an easy way to find out. Just look at your surroundings and realize that you—through your thoughts and beliefs—have created that. Whether you're living in a great environment or a not-so-good environment, you have created that environment with your belief window.

Universal laws

I believe that there are universal laws that everybody needs to understand. They have been around forever, and whether you believe in them or not, they are working in your life every day.

These universal laws exist today for each of us. They literally will govern your success, your failure, and your relationships. They're real, even though a lot of people don't believe in them. The sad part about that, for those non-believers, is that those laws still affect their lives every day. Sometimes people will blame things on bad luck. They'll say, "I never get a break" or "Things always go against me." It has nothing to do with any of that. It's about the fact that they're violating some of those universal laws.

What do I mean by universal laws? They are the laws that deal with energy, with light and darkness. They go back to the formation of the universe, to when this earth was formed. You may have your own beliefs about how that came to be. Personally, I believe in a higher power. For me that higher power is God. You may call it a higher power; you may call it the divine spirit; you may call it what you will. Whatever we call it, it is the source of these universal laws.

Maybe the easiest universal laws to understand are the physical ones, like the law of gravity, or the laws of thermodynamics. You'll find those in any science book.

Here's another universal law: the law of attraction. The essence of the law of attraction is that what you put out to the universe comes back to you. Positive energy attracts positive; negative energy attracts negative. The law of attraction is probably the most important for people to really study, comprehend, and use.

Why is that so important? Remember your belief window: the world as you experience it is formed by your beliefs. If those beliefs are negative, and you are putting out negative energy because of them, the law of attraction tells you that you will attract negative energy.

And what if those negative beliefs are false? I've heard it said that scientists estimate that up to 77 percent of everything on the belief window is false or no longer serves a purpose. Think about that for a moment. What if you were out in the middle of the ocean on a big luxury liner and you heard the captain say, "Ladies and gentlemen, I'm sorry to inform you that the computer system that's running this ship is operating on information that is 77 percent false." Would that make you a little nervous? I believe it would. So why would you want to live your life based on such false information?

I can hear you saying, "But you said all those messages stay on my belief window. So what can I do about it?"

Cleaning your window

The good news is that you **can** do something to change that.

Is it easy? No. Why is it so hard for us to change? First of all, we don't believe we can. Secondly, we get ourselves trapped in a box. We allow ourselves to get comfortable there because it's easier than taking up the hard work of change.

It takes courage, but you can do it. You start by taking that window out, putting it on the table, and examining the beliefs that you hold and that you have written yourself on that window. Let's find which of those beliefs still serve you and which ones do not. When we do, we can take some Windex and some towels and scrub that window clean. We can get rid of the pessimism and self-doubt that go with those negative beliefs and instead put up new beliefs that better serve us.

You can take the bad beliefs off and replace them with better beliefs. Then all of a sudden, when you're looking out at the world, it's a much brighter, shinier, more wonderful place. Here's the amazing part: It is in your control. It is your choice. You get to choose what's on that window. It's wonderful!

2. Burn Your Ships

*Commitment is what turns a promise
into reality.*
Abraham Lincoln

In the year 1519, the Spanish conquistador Hernán Cortés landed in what is now Mexico. He was an ambitious man, determined to conquer the Aztec nation that then occupied the region. How determined was he? Once all of his troops were on the shore, he ordered all of their ships destroyed. He told his men they would conquer or die.

Cortés had fewer than 600 men. The Aztec nation had thousands upon thousands of warriors. Yet history tells us that the Aztecs fell to Cortés and his small Spanish force. How was that even possible? One big reason was that Cortés' men had no choice. There was no going back home. They had to win or perish.

No escape

I've always been a history buff, and I like to use this story as an example in business and in life. I think it's important to point out that all too often, people leave themselves an escape route. What do I mean by escape route? It's what I call the "Yeah, but." "Yeah but, if this had happened …" "Yeah, but if I had done that …" "Yeah, but if we had gotten …" All the excuses that you could ever imagine are part of the escape route.

Let's be clear. When I say "burn your ships," I am not saying burn every relationship you've ever had or burn everything you've ever done. That's not what I'm talking about. I'm talking about burning your escape route. If you really want to do something, you need to plant a flagpole and say, "This is where I'm going to make my stand. This is what I'm going to be known for. This is the success that I'm going to create." You've got to burn the escape routes so that the first time you run into hard times—and you will—you don't fall back and say, "Oh well, let me go find something else. This is a little harder than I thought; maybe it'll be easier over there."

If you leave yourself an escape route, I promise you that you'll probably use it. If you burn those ships and leave no escape from what you say is your goal—from what you desire amongst all desires—you'll find a way to achieve it and you'll stop looking for the escape routes.

I have seen this so many times in my network marketing and home-based business career, in other businesses and even life in general. I've watched so many people do the same thing. They say that this is what they want, they set their goal, and then the minute things get a little tough, they quit. They realize that this goal they've created is going to be a lot of work. It's not as easy as they thought it was going to be.

Guess what? It never is.

That's when the shiny objects start to look appealing. They look to be easier. I can tell you this: There's always a new shiny object out there that can distract you from your goal. Then all of a sudden, whether it's in your relationships or your family life, or your business life, it's easy to get distracted, get off target, and go chase something else.

So often, people go off chasing another dream when they were so close to achieving their original goal. They never realized how close they've come. There are countless stories about people who quit just as they were about to achieve their goal.

There's a classic story about this called *Acres of Diamonds*. Earl Nightingale used to tell the story frequently, but it can be traced back to a speech by Dr. Russell H. Conwell, the founder of Temple University. Conwell died in 1925, but during his lifetime, by his own count, he delivered his Acres of Diamonds speech more than 6,000 times!

It's the supposedly true story of an African farmer who became obsessed with diamonds. Although his farm was prosperous, he dreamed of finding diamonds that would make him incredibly wealthy. He sold his farm, left his family, and took off in search of diamonds. He traveled far and wide for years, but never found the diamonds he was seeking. Eventually, broke and discouraged, he threw himself into a river and drowned.

Meanwhile, the man who had bought the farm from him discovered that the farm itself was full of diamonds. It became one of the richest mines the world had ever seen. The farmer never realized that he had been standing in his own "acres of diamonds" all along.

How often do we do that? How often do we overlook what is right beneath our feet?

The point is that you don't quit on your goal. Remember Tom Hanks as the coach in "A League of Their Own?" When his players complained, he said, "It's supposed to be hard. If it wasn't hard, everyone would do it. The hard ... is what makes it great."

It's difficult, but it's supposed to be difficult. If it weren't difficult everybody would be doing it. It is a noble endeavor to go after your goal and each of us gets to pick our own goals. Don't get distracted by a shiny object that looks easier once you realize your goal has work attached to it. The old saying claims that the grass is always greener on the other side. But when you get to the other side, you will realize that it's not. It's still work over there just like it was work over here. I do a lot of work in the area of home-based business, and I see that it usually happens somewhere from 30 to 90 days after someone starts their home-based business. They leave one company, thinking that an opportunity with another company will be easier, and about 60 days after they get there, they realize it's not. It's still work.

The challenge is this: Is the work worth it? For me, absolutely. For you? You tell me; it's your goal. How badly do you really want it? If you truly desire your goal then burn the escape route so that you stay committed to it and keep working through the hardships to achieve it.

Staying the course: Cindy's story

One of the best examples I know of being committed to a goal is my wife, Cindy. She worked in the corporate office of the school district for quite a few years; she had also worked in outside businesses. She finally decided that she wanted to make a bigger difference in kids' lives. She knew she couldn't do that behind her desk at corporate. So she went back to school to get her college degree. She went back to school while working a full-time job and at the same time raising a family. It was very difficult. The sacrifice was endless. She put in years of studying at night—till two or three o'clock in the morning—to complete her degree. It was nine years of taking one or two classes at a time for her to finish her bachelor's and then her masters.

The point is that today, every day, she's making a difference in the lives of the kids she teaches.

It would have been easier for her to stay put. She was making more money before she became a teacher. But her goal was bigger. She had seen what a difference a teacher could make, especially for kids who had some challenges. She had always wanted to be a teacher, but we got married and had kids, and she was also working. It wasn't convenient for her to go back to school.

So during those nine years, she had plenty of "Yeah, but" moments. She could have quit many times but she had technically burned her escape routes. She had made up her mind what she wanted. She wanted to make a difference and that was the way she believed she could do it. She never let all the excuses she could have found get in the way, and she achieved the goal she had set herself.

You can do the same. Marshall Ferdinand Foch once said, "The most powerful weapon on earth is the human soul on fire." What's the goal that sets your soul on fire?

3. Leave No Doubt

We are not interested in the possibilities
of defeat; they do not exist.
Queen Victoria

Do you remember the movie "Remember the Titans?" If you haven't seen it, I recommend it. It's a great sports movie with some great lessons for life. In the movie, which is based on a true story, the Titans are a high school football team that has gone through some tough times. At one point, they're playing in a championship game against an opponent whose behavior has generally been what I would call unsportsmanlike, even including some very personal insults from the opposing coaches.

Early in the game, the Titans are behind, but once they finally get on the scoreboard, they tie it up and then score to take the lead. As they move ahead, the assistant coach hollers over to Herman, the head coach, saying, "Run it up, Herman. Leave no doubt." They were going to send a clear message to the other team that their comments and insults were unacceptable.

Now, as a side note, let me make it clear that in my coaching days, I never ran up the score intentionally. I never wanted to embarrass the other team. I don't believe in that. I understand that part of coaching and I understand why they ran it up in this case, but it's not something I would do myself.

Running up the score is not important. What is important is this: Leave no doubt in anyone's mind about what you believe.

Do you *really* believe?

Whatever you're attempting to do, you need to buy into it heart, body, and soul. People will hear your belief in your voice and they will see it in your body language. People need to feel your words. That's what I want to do with this book. I don't want you to just read these words. I want you to feel the passion and the belief behind these words I'm sharing with you. That's why I'm doing this, because I believe so wholeheartedly that these lessons I've learned can help you to succeed in changing your life for the better, personally or professionally.

If you're working in sales, for instance, and you attempt to show somebody what you're selling, you'd better be proud of what you're selling. Whether they buy from you or not, whether they join your cause or not, when they walk away from you, they have to walk away saying, wow, that man, that woman, that person absolutely believes in what they're talking about.

If you're talking on the telephone, you have to have that excitement, that passion, and that energy in your voice. It's contagious. People pick up on it.

If you're meeting in person, you have to have that same excitement along with the corresponding body language. You stand a little taller. You hold your head high; you put your shoulders back. You need to be completely into what you're talking about with people.

Belief is contagious

Let me share with you a couple of personal stories to show you what I mean. Early in my coaching years, I took over a team that nobody wanted. They'd only won two games in two years. They were terrible. Everyone I knew said, "Barry, what are you doing? Are you crazy?" It made no sense to them, because in my first year my friend Don Anhder and I had coached a championship team with some other kids.

I knew the first thing I had to do was turn the mentality around. When I started talking about championships to kids who were so down and out, it was hard for them. At first, they couldn't stretch their minds enough to believe they could win. I had to turn their thought process around. The one thing that they did believe was that Barry McLeod absolutely believed in what he was talking about. I made sure there was no doubt in any of their minds about that. We just had to work on them believing it and we did. I showed them they couldn't get there by just sitting around watching TV. Their success came by getting off the couch, turning the TV off, and going to work.

Was it worth it in the end? I believe it was. I still have kids from way back then who stay in contact with me, because when they played for me, they learned how to win. They learned how to clean off their belief window and put new beliefs on it. And then, for the first time in their lives, they had the opportunity to know—even for just one moment— that they were the best of the best. It turned their lives around. That's what this is all about: putting hope back into people and helping them understand that they have more potential than they realize.

It works. It absolutely works. I saw it work over and over again in sports, and then I learned how to make it work in business as well. While I'd had great success in the sports arena, I'd had a hard time transferring that success into the business world. I couldn't understand why. I knew it should work. Then I finally got an opportunity to prove it.

From sports to business

My mother was working at a car rental agency that was really struggling. It was near bankruptcy and the owner was ready to close it. I met with the owner and said to him, "I think we can change this. I believe I can change it." He said, "How?" I told him, "I'm going to run this like a ball team—just like all the successful championship teams I've coached." He was intrigued by that, and so he hired me as the new general manager.

Looking back, I know that he really had nothing to lose, since the company was going under anyway. The day I walked through the door, I got nothing but resentment from the other employees. They all felt that the general manager should have been someone promoted from within the agency. They thought it should have been one of them, not some outsider. I toured each of the agency's three offices, and the resentment was obvious.

It was bad. No one wanted to take responsibility for the fact that the agency was in such bad shape because of them and their poor work ethic. Employee morale was pitiful. The cars were even more pitiful—most of them were beat-up junkers with holes in the seats and 100,000 miles on them.

My first thought was, okay, how did I turn my ball teams around? I realized that I needed to change the company mentality and change the thought process. I gathered all the employees together and had my first meeting. I told them what we were going to do, and I said, "I need your help to do this."

In the entire company there were only three people that I knew would be with me, and I had three offices to worry about. I don't think anybody believed what I said that night. But remember what I said about leaving no doubt?

There was no doubt in their minds that I believed what I was saying. So we went to work.

Every time some businessman came in to rent from us, I personally walked out to the car with him. I would say, "Mr. Businessman, I know this car is not up to your expectations. I know that you can go somewhere else and get something better. But if you'll just stick with me and give me the opportunity to turn this around, I promise you the day will come that you will be renting a much nicer car from us at still the best prices in town." I taught all of our salespeople to do the same thing. Because we added such a personal touch, a lot of customers stayed with us month after month while we were turning the company around.

Every Thursday night we had a weekly staff meeting. Everyone was required to be there. It was part of turning around the company mentality. I taught my ball-playing philosophy and some of the motivational lessons I had learned. One Thursday during the day, I fired one of the managers. He was the owner's favorite, by the way, but I had good reason to fire him. That night, at the start of the meeting, one of the outside salesmen, stood up in front of the entire company—including me—and told everybody, to my face, that Barry McLeod was crazy.

I'd been called crazy a lot of times in my coaching days, so that didn't bother me. But he told everybody there that the company was done. That Barry had fired the best manager they'd ever had. That Barry was a bad leader.

I kept my cool. I just said, "I'm sorry you feel that way about it. There's the door; you can pick up your final check tomorrow." And he left.

Then I had a meeting with the people who were left. I told them again the vision that I had for the company and the work that it was going to take to do it. I said, "If you want to stay with me and do this, I'm leaving a pencil and tablet here on this counter. You sign your name to it. I'm going to be back in about two hours after everybody's gone. Those of you who have signed, I'll expect you to be here tomorrow to help build this dream. Those of you who don't, I totally understand and we'll make your final checks available."

As far as I knew, there were only three people in that room who would back me and those three wouldn't be enough to run all three offices the next day. I thought, wow, the owner's going to go ballistic; I've just fired his manager and here we go.

So when I left that night, I was really sweating bullets. I drove around for a while, then I watched from a distance as everybody left and they closed up the office. All I could think about was how I was going to run the company the next day if everybody left.

When I came back two hours later, I found that all but one of the employees had signed the paper. But that night was an example of leaving no doubt. Sometimes in life, to achieve your dream, you have to go way out on a limb. When you're out on that limb, you leave no doubt in anybody's mind that the dream is going to happen. What I was saying to the employees that night was this: "With or without you, I'm going to make this happen. This dream of mine is that special."

I think that night we reached that turning point where people finally said to themselves, "This guy's serious. He believes in this. I think I'm going to stick around." So from that point forward we worked our tails off, and things started to happen.

It didn't come easy. We went through 93 people in that first year, not because I was so hard to work for, but because I was looking for team players.

We were broke. I didn't have the money to offer anyone more than minimum wage. But we needed people who would be <u>believers</u>—people who would be crusaders for this grand vision that I had about having the best car rental company in the whole valley.

How did I attract those people? I recruited them. When I was coaching ball teams, I'd drive around the area that we were allowed to recruit from. I'd find kids who were playing ball out in the street and I'd pull over to watch them. If I saw talent there, I'd go talk to them about coming out for our team. I did the same thing with the car rental agency.

One summer day, for example, I was driving to the office and I saw a girls' car wash going on. I pulled over across the street and I sat and watched them for a good half hour. Most of the girls were standing around talking, but there were two girls who were really working hard. I went over to them and gave them both my card. I said, "I admire your work ethic. If you'd like a job for this summer, come and see me." They both did. We hired them and they played a key part in helping turn things around for us. All through high school, they worked for our company.

We took every opportunity to build our team. For example, we were the first car rental agency in the Las Vegas Valley to sell extra insurance. It's common practice now to buy extra insurance when you rent a car, but it wasn't in those days.

I received a proposal from an insurance company that offered a bonus payment for every policy we sold. I thought the extra insurance would be a good thing for our customers, so at our next Thursday meeting, I explained the proposal to our staff. I told them that for every policy we sold, we would take the payments and divide them equally. Every Thursday night we would divide up that week's payment. Everyone got the same amount, from the car washers to me, the general manager. It helped everyone to understand that it wasn't all about me. It was about the dream of becoming the best rental agency around. It worked. It worked very well.

At one point, another rental agency moved in right across the street from us. They were big. They had nicer cars, and they had more money behind them than we did. Their manager tried to make a deal with me. He told me that if I would make sure that all his cars were rented first, then he would give us his overflow.

I said thanks but no thanks and told him that we would keep on doing what we had been doing. He scoffed at me and left. One day, some months later, I was out in the back washing cars when one of my people came out and said, "Barry, you've got to come and see this."

I followed him out front and we all watched as trucks loaded up all the other agency's cars and took them away. We actually outlasted them. Why? Because we out-worked them and we out-believed them. We didn't give up on our dream.

At the end of seven years, we had the best car rental agency in town. We did have nicer, newer cars. We still had a lot of the original customers who stayed with us through the thick and thin. We still gave them the best prices in town. We were taking business away from Hertz, and Avis, and Alamo, and all the rest. And we also had money to give raises to all the people who stayed with us. It was a lot of work, but what we created together was incredible. In the process, I proved to myself that I could run a business like a ball team and succeed.

Share your dream

What I learned from my years in coaching ball teams is that people—I think it's human nature—want to belong to something bigger than they are. They want to belong to a cause, or a crusade, or a dream that looks impossible. Once they buy into it and truly believe in it, they'll work their hearts out.

You can't sell the dream if you're not a dreamer yourself. You can't sell the dream unless you believe in the dream yourself with your heart, body, and soul. You can't sell the dream if it's all about being selfish. It wasn't all about me; that's why we shared the bonus money. That's why the general manager and the manager were out washing cars. That's why we praised the car washers as much as we praised anybody else. We were a team.

As I said earlier, it's all about belief. When you believe in what you're doing, and when your body language, your tone of voice, your passion, and your energy, convey that belief—when you leave no doubt—you attract other believers to you. In the same way, losing teams or losing organizations, that offer only blame and excuses, tend to keep attracting those who won't take responsibility for their actions and their results. Therefore, they never get anywhere. **The world belongs to the believers**.

4. W. Clement Stone and the Hundredth Monkey

All I want to do is change the world,
make it a better place for this
and future generations.
W. Clement Stone

I'll bet most of you reading this book have never heard the name W. Clement Stone. I think that's a shame, because he is one of my biggest heroes.

When W. Clement Stone died in 2002 at the age of 100, the headline in the *New York Times* obituary claimed that he had "built an empire on optimism." He was an entrepreneur, a businessman and a philanthropist who built a multimillion dollar insurance company starting from just a hundred dollars in savings.

In his 1962 book, *A Success System That Never Fails*, he tells the story of how he got started in business, as a little kid selling newspapers. Bigger kids kept pushing him out of the prime spots, so he went into local restaurants where patrons were having their breakfast, and started selling newspapers in there. When a restaurant owner tried to run him out, he just kept coming back until the owner finally gave up. Imagine the courage and persistence that took for a little kid!

The other amazing thing about W. Clement Stone is that he actually created his insurance empire during the Great Depression of the 1930s. At a time when most Americans were standing in the soup line or the bread line, he was going door to door selling accident insurance. This is what I mean when I say all things are possible: W. Clement Stone is a great example. During the Great Depression, this man created an empire.

Let me tell you how I came to learn about W. Clement Stone.

Starting over

It seems unbelievable now, but I actually spent 11 years working in an industry that I really didn't like. I was a dispatcher for an automobile dealership, and one of the people in charge was a real bully. He was always berating the employees. He usually left me alone because he didn't know much about dispatching, but one day, for some unknown reason, he decided to pick on me.

He came into the office and started giving me a hard time. I was fed up after watching him do this time and time again to other people, so when he started on me I refused to take it. I told him, "If you think you can do this better than me, here it is. Take over." All of the crew were standing there watching the confrontation; you could have heard a pin drop in the silence. He knew he couldn't take over the dispatch office, because he didn't know how, so he stormed out. I took a stand for myself and all the other employees that he'd been mistreating for years.

You probably won't be surprised to learn that when I came to work the next day, I was informed that I no longer had a job. Well, anytime you're let loose or fired, there's a sense of panic: "Oh my goodness, I've got a wife and two kids, what am I going to do?" At that time mine was the only source of income we had. Then of course there was the embarrassment of having to tell people that I had been fired.

As difficult as that experience is for anyone, it can actually turn out to be a blessing in disguise. It was for me. It was one of the best things that ever happened to me. How can that be, you ask? This is how: It got me out of an industry that I hated; it got me out of the golden handcuffs. When you've been working in the same place for a while, after you've had a few raises, you start to tell yourself, "I can't start over somewhere else because I can't go back down to the bottom of the pay scale. We've got a family and we've got bills to pay." It's how you get trapped into a job you've come to hate.

Obviously, I needed to find a new job quickly, and I was looking everywhere when a newspaper ad caught my eye. It said, "Are you sports-minded? Do you like to play as a team?" I thought, man, that's me! Even though the ad didn't say what the job was, I went down to apply. There was a whole room full of people applying for this mysterious job. We each took a little test and filled out some paperwork. I still didn't know what the job was. We all came back the second day. They separated out all the people whose applications they rejected, and then the room was about half full. We came back the third day, and that's when I actually found out that the job was selling insurance for the Combined Insurance Company, which was owned by W. Clement Stone.

I was picked and they sent me up to Salt Lake City for two weeks of training. When I first got there, it was overwhelming. I can't even describe the huge stack of pages that we had to memorize word for word. My first thought, of course, was that I'd never be able to do this. I couldn't memorize all of this. But over the next two weeks, in an environment that was completely positive and uplifting, I accomplished what I thought was impossible. I learned about W. Clement Stone and his book, *The Success System That Never Fails*. We all studied that book.

It was such a positive environment for me because even after winning so many championships as a coach and as a player, up until that point I had not been able to really transfer that success into the business world. It was a puzzle to me, and of course spending 11 years in a job I didn't like made it even harder. W. Clement Stone was really big on what we now call affirmations. Every morning you'd get up and you'd say your chants. You'd say your cheers, and you'd be looking at yourself in the mirror, just psyching yourself up for the day. It was an unbelievably positive environment. There were no impossibilities there; there were no negatives. It was uplifting, and more importantly, it was contagious. I saw how that kind of environment can take people to another level if you have the ability to create that kind of environment for them.

When I left there at the end of the two weeks, of course I was excited to come back to my family, but part of me was sad to be leaving that environment. I realized that the environment I found at that school was the same environment that we had created building those winning ball teams. I made up my mind that wherever I go, I've got to create that environment.

Once I got home, I needed to take the insurance test. At the time the state of Nevada had the hardest insurance test in the nation. I had to take it twice, but I finally passed and got my license to get out into the field. It was hard work. Anyone who's ever gone cold-calling all day long, door to door, business to business, can tell you what hard work it is. It can be scary, it can be frightening, and it's tough. But I used the W. Clement Stone philosophy I had learned, and I had some success with it. I was there for a couple of years.

When I finally left, I took the W. Clement Stone philosophy and transferred it to the car rental agency I described earlier. I taught that philosophy in our weekly Thursday night meetings. We lived and worked with that philosophy.

The main point is this: If W. Clement Stone could build an insurance empire during the Great Depression, then what is holding you back from what you would like to build for your own life? I sometimes hear people say, "Well, the economy's bad." So what? The economy was horrible when W. Clement Stone built his business. It couldn't have been any worse.

Don't rely on excuses. One of the W. Clement Stone sayings we memorized was "Do it now. Do it now. Do it now." Don't hesitate. I'll give you an example. We were taught that it didn't matter whether it was a big bank or a little mom and pop store. If it was on your street, you were going to knock on that door and go in.

One day, I came to an insurance agency. Of course I was selling insurance, but I'd been trained to "do it now." I got past the secretary to see the owner of that agency. He was at his big desk, so I sat down and proceeded with my presentation. He stopped me and said, "Son, I have to ask you a question. Do you know where you're at?" I said, "Yes, I do." He said, "Well, you're attempting to sell me insurance and I am an insurance agency." I said, "I understand that."

What he did next was a good lesson for me. He said, "I want you to have my card. Anybody that has the guts to come in here selling insurance, if you ever leave that company, I want you to come work for us." When you're following this "success system that never fails," you never know what doors are going to open for you, but you have to have the courage to follow the system. You have to knock on that door and go through it.

It takes courage and it means you might have to be willing to look foolish, which brings me to one of my favorite stories about W. Clement Stone. At one time, his company's sales in London were really pitiful, so W. Clement Stone himself got on a plane and flew to London.

I should tell you that when I worked for his company, we met as a team every morning. There was a pep talk, we did our rituals to psych ourselves up, and then we each had different assignments. We'd be told where to go and which streets we were covering. So when W. Clement Stone got to London, he gathered together every one of his agents who were covering the city. For an entire day he had them march in unison up and down the streets of London singing their cheers, and their chants, and their "do it now" and other things that Stone had taught them. They did that for an entire day! Now, what did that accomplish? Well, by the end of that day, everyone in London knew about Combined Insurance Company and W. Clement Stone's sales team there. And the phenomenal thing was that sales skyrocketed.

Now, did it take courage to take a group of people and march them up and down the streets singing and chanting? Of course it did. Did they get strange looks? Of course they did. Did people say they were crazy? Of course they did. But did they accomplish what they set out to do? Absolutely! Their sales started to skyrocket because all of a sudden people were aware of W. Clement Stone.

Stone understood the importance of that awareness. There's a critical tipping point that's reached in building awareness, in building a company, in building a team. One way to describe that tipping point is the hundredth monkey theory.

The hundredth monkey

When I mention the hundredth monkey in my presentations, most people just give me strange looks. They've never heard of the story. Ken Keyes Jr. describes it in his book *The Hundredth Monkey*, but here's a brief summary.

Back in the 1950s, scientists were studying monkeys on an island in the Pacific. They found that the monkeys loved sweet potatoes so every day they would drop the sweet potatoes off on the shore and then they'd observe them.

The monkeys loved the potatoes, but because they were dropped on the shore, sand stuck to the potatoes and although the monkeys would eat them, the sand would be scratching their throats. One day a baby monkey—just one baby monkey—took her sweet potato over to a nearby river and washed it off and ate it. The scientists observed that while the baby monkey was doing that, all the other monkeys were watching and pointing, as if they were laughing. But the next day they noticed a couple more of the baby monkeys washed off their potatoes and the day after that, even more did the same thing.

The experiment went on for several years. Eventually some of the adults started washing their potatoes. Eventually it became the practice for all of the monkeys. The book says they don't know if it was the hundredth monkey or the two-hundredth, but the point is that there was a tipping point. Let's say 99 of the monkeys were washing their potatoes, then the next day, when one more monkey—the hundredth monkey—did it, the following day the whole island was doing it. What's so strange about that? Here's what shocked the scientists: When that hundredth monkey picked up the potato and went over and rinsed it off, the same phenomenon began to happen on other islands as well.

Ken Keyes describes it this way:

> "When a certain critical number achieves awareness, this new awareness may be communicated from mind to mind. All while the exact number may vary, the hundredth monkey phenomenon means that when only one, when only a limited number of people know of a new way, it may remain the conscious property of those people but there is a point at which if only one more

person tunes in to a new awareness, a field is strengthened so that this awareness is picked up by almost everyone. In other words, it goes from mind to mind."

You may choose whether or not to accept the hundredth monkey theory, but here's what I've found. There's always a tipping point. You may think you're alone in your efforts to make a difference out there but as you recruit other people to join your crusade, there comes a time when enough people have banded together with the same thought process that now that consciousness is actually transferred to other people. Never think that you're by yourself out there. You don't know where that tipping point is. If you just bring one more person to your cause, to your crusade, to your business, that individual could be the mythical hundredth monkey that means suddenly everyone knows about your cause.

I'll give you an example. I have a very good friend, George Antarr, who always tells this story. When he was a young kid just out of college, he couldn't find a job anywhere. He answered an ad in the paper and it was for a network marketing company that sold weight loss products.

He joined the company, started selling the products, and made a small fortune. As he tells it now, he thought that his success was due to his being good-looking and a great salesman, with a gift for talking to people. He didn't realize until years later that it had nothing to do with any of that.

What happened was that he joined the company just as the awareness expanded everywhere and all of a sudden everybody wanted his products.

George is very humble about that, but the point of his story is that timing is everything. In your life, in your project, or in your crusade, you never, ever know when adding just one more person will make the difference. I love George and his wife Dr. Donna not only for the huge success they have attained, but also for the thousands of people they have helped along the way.

In my own life, I can cite the examples of building the car rental agency or building all of those winning ball teams. In each case, when I first got there, the consciousness was horrible. Nobody wanted to work at the rental agency; nobody wanted to be on that ball team. But as we gathered crusaders, it was the same principle. Once we added just that one person—that hundredth monkey—all of a sudden the consciousness of the entire team or the entire company changed and we began to attract people who wanted to be a part of what we were doing. Maybe you had to be there. Maybe you had to see it to believe it, but I can tell you this principle is true. In whatever you're attempting to do, you're never alone.

Another of my favorite movies illustrates what I've been saying in this chapter. Have you ever seen *The Magnificent Seven*? It's an old western with Yul Brynner and Steve

McQueen. I love that movie. It's inspirational to me and here's why. When Yul Brynner takes on the task of defending a village, he needs help so he goes around gathering others to his cause. He can't pay anybody—which reminds me of my car rental business because I couldn't pay anybody either—but he gathers Steve McQueen and some others to the cause. Every time they would pick up one more person, they'd hold up a finger. First one, then two, then three, and then eventually they had seven people who went and defended the village. I think of the seventh person in that situation as the equivalent of the hundredth monkey.

The point is that it's easier to attract people once that consciousness has been established. This principle works in the opposite direction, too. If your attitude is always "woe is me" or "yeah, but ...", or you are making every excuse in the world, you will attract people who are the same.

It's all about work, and it's all about believing in yourself and your cause. I know for certain that these principles work; I've seen them work in every aspect of my own life. Now let's talk about how you can put these principles to work in your life and work.

5. Input

The human brain will do
anything possible you tell it to do,
if you tell it often enough
and strongly enough!
Shad Helmstetter

In the last chapters, I've shared some personal stories and stories that have inspired me. I hope they have inspired you to want to change your own story.

Let's talk about you. What practical steps can you take to start changing your life? How do you start rewriting your story?

Remember what we said about your belief window? Every day, you are adding new information to your belief window. That information comes from many sources: newspapers, television, radio, family, friends, and increasingly, from the internet and social media. Whenever you take in information, whatever the source, it's being added to your belief window. Unfortunately, a lot of that is negative information. Each of us needs to learn to filter out the negative information and take in the positive information instead. That can be very difficult in this world that we live in. It usually doesn't happen by accident. You're going to have to go out of your way to eliminate negative information and replace it with positive input. How are you going to do that?

Eliminate the negative, accentuate the positive

One way to do that is to get yourself some positive motivational books or audiobooks. If you live in an area where they are available, go to motivational seminars. This is your life and you need to be very protective of it. All of the negative messages that you are exposed to every day really do have an influence on the decisions you're making about your life.

In Chapter 1 we talked about the human brain as a computer. The negative messages you take in are constantly typing on that computer's keyboard.

For instance, as I told you earlier, when I was growing up, I was too thin. I was not good at sports. Those were the messages I was typing into my brain. "Barry's too thin." "Barry's not very good at sports." It's important to understand that once that input is received into the computer/brain, it can't be deleted. So you need to use the delete key on those negative messages before they ever get in there. You need to learn how to override those negative messages before they can make it to your belief window.

Negative messages don't just come from external sources, though. Your own self-talk—what you tell yourself about what you can and can't do—also contributes to your belief window. Many of us get into the habit of negative self-talk, and we need to learn how to break that habit.

Changing your self-talk

Dr. Shad Helmstetter, who is a pioneer and expert in the art of self-talk, or the science of self-talk, points out that most of what we tell ourselves is negative. He has written a number of books, including the classic *What to Say When You Talk to Yourself.*

The human brain contains millions of neurons. Dr. Helmstetter explains that our self-talk forms what he calls "superhighways" from those neurons. For instance, suppose that you are in sales and you're having a hard time cold-calling. All of a sudden, your boss says, "Today we're going out cold-calling." Your first reaction is to tell yourself, "I'm not good at this. I've never been good at this. I don't like this. I'm going to be imposing on people and they're not going to want to hear what I have to say." The more emotion or energy you put behind that thought, the deeper it drives into your brain, and the more it starts to form these superhighways.

Sure enough, with that negative thought process, you're going to go out there and have another miserable day cold-calling. It's science. It can't be any other way. And what has happened is you've just created a self-fulfilling prophecy that adds to your negative belief. At the end of the day, you've just added more negative input into your thought process. What happens next? Here's how it works. Suppose the next day is your day off. Your spouse tells you that it's time to clean out the attic, or mow the lawn, or weed the garden. Whatever it is, it's something you don't really want to do that day. Instantly that superhighway engages. All those neurons fire together again and you feel the same emotion that you had yesterday about cold-calling.

Now that same emotion is about cleaning out the attic, and within nanoseconds, those neurons are firing together and taking you down that very same superhighway. That means you're in for an experience that won't be good. You tell yourself, "Maybe I'm going to clean the attic out, but I'm not going to like it and I'm going to be grumbling the whole time and this is going to be a miserable day off." Then the next day, for some reason, you're stuck in traffic, and instantly you're saying to yourself, "Oh, why do I live here? Why do I put up with this traffic? What is that buffoon up in front of me doing?" And sure enough, all those neurons fire together, and that same emotion rises. The same neurons that were all negative about the cold-calling, the same neurons that were all negative about cleaning the attic, are now firing together because you're stuck in traffic.

You end up having another miserable experience and it just adds deeper and deeper levels to this negative superhighway. As simple as this sounds, this really is the way it works. What can you do about it?

You can override that negative highway if you want to, when you understand how it affects your life every day. How much do you want to do that? It is possible to get stuck in traffic and laugh about it and have a good time. It is possible to clean out the attic and make it an enjoyable experience with your spouse. It is possible to go out cold-calling and at the end of the day say, "Wow, I'm getting better at this."

How did you get better at it, by the way? Was it because you picked up some skills? Yes, but the big reason you got better is that you changed your thought process.

Rerouting the superhighway

Let's talk a bit more about that thought process. There is a small part of your brain called the **Reticular Activating System, or RAS**. This RAS has a number of important functions. It helps to regulate sleep, waking, and the ability to focus attention. That last one is very important. What that means is that the RAS regulates what and how you notice things. You are constantly being bombarded by external and internal stimuli. The RAS sifts through all those stimuli and determines what gets through to your conscious mind. It acts as a filter to keep your senses from getting overloaded.

What's important about this is that whether you know it or not, your RAS filters the information it receives based on your beliefs. It works to make sure that the world you see around you matches the world you hold inside you, that is, your belief window. The RAS makes sure that your outside world picture matches your inside world picture.

Here's a simple example. Suppose you decide to buy a yellow Volkswagen bug. You choose it because (a) it stands out, and (b) it's unique. You've never seen one before. But all of a sudden, now that you've driving this yellow Volkswagen, it seems as though all you see as you're driving down the freeway are more yellow Volkswagens. They were there all along. Your RAS just didn't pick them up because they weren't on your mind or in your consciousness.

Here's another example. If your belief window is loaded with negative messages, if you're carrying around baggage from 20 years ago when somebody offended you and you've never gotten over it, your RAS is going to find more negative messages wherever you go. If you're carrying all that negativity inside, your RAS, looking at your outside world, will find circumstances to match what's inside you.

It doesn't matter where you are. If you're in the grocery store or you're at the mall—wherever you are—you're going to find a sales clerk you think is rude, or someone will bump into you, or something else will offend you or rub you the wrong way. Then you say to yourself, "Well, I'm never going back to that store; that sales clerk was horrible." It's not the sales clerk; it's you. You put that together and you are responsible for it.

Let's take the opposite view. Let's say you're feeling on top of the world. Everything's going your way. You're excited, you're happy, you've got good things happening. Your RAS is looking at the outside world, and is going to bring more of that happiness into your life, because that's what its instructions are. That's its programming: "I've got a happy fellow, or I've got a happy lady here, so everything is going her way." Some talk about luck. I don't believe in luck. It's all about your RAS. You created the luck, whether it's bad or good. You created it with your thoughts, and your belief window. That gets transferred to the RAS, which looks at the outside world, finds a match, and brings it back to you.

This is an area of science that fascinates me; I could spend days talking about it. If you'd like to know more about it, I encourage you to do some additional reading or internet searching; there's a lot of information out there. The main thing that I want you to understand is that you are in charge of your life.

The law of attraction

Thoughts are real, be they good or bad. They are real, and they will attract to you the same energy or lack of energy that you put out into the world.

These days there's a lot of discussion about the law of attraction. Some believe that it is a mystical thing. I believe it's real, but I'm not convinced it's mystical. I believe the Law of Attraction is all about the RAS. I think it all has to do with your brain, and your RAS, as it functions to make good and sure that your outside world matches your inside world. If you think that you're going to change your outside world into positive success, whether in your love life, your relationships, or your business, and still carry around all the negative junk inside you, you're just fooling yourself. It's not going to happen. You will run into road block, after road block, after road block.

You have to change your thought process first. When we turned those ball teams around, and turned that rental agency around, and when we've turned around individuals whom we've mentored and coached, the first thing we always had to do was change the mental process. Change the mental picture. Take that belief window off. Examine the beliefs that are there, and the ones that no longer serve us, or you, or them, get rid of them. Put new and better beliefs there. It really is that simple.

Remember our Kody Bateman quote from Chapter 1: "The stories in your mind become the stories of your life." The good news is this: We get to choose our own stories. Some readers may have a hard time comprehending that, but I promise you, if you will accept that as fact, and start working on it, you will see miraculous changes in your life.

I have no doubt in my mind about that. I've seen it work time and time again.

Beyond our control?

Some people will say, "Wait, I have this disease. That's not something I can control." It's true that there are some circumstances that are beyond our control—disease, injury, our backgrounds, even other people's choices. What we can control is how we choose to react to these circumstances. Some might even ask whether they might have attracted this disease to themselves. I don't believe that at all. Disease is a sad and horrible situation. I do say that how we accept such bad news is up to us. Medical science offers new advances every day, and there is plenty of evidence that the course of treatment or even recovery can be affected by the patient's mental and emotional outlook. Someone who is positive, upbeat, and refuses to get beat often has a better outcome. I believe completely that that our thoughts can improve our bodily situation.

How many times have you seen someone retire, and then sit around and do nothing? The next thing you know they're gone. But other people retire, and they're not ready to go; they're not ready to sit around and do nothing. They start a new project, or set a new goal in life. Those people tend to live a lot longer. Why? It's because of their thought process. It's because they've put a new dream, or a new hope, into their lives, and they've gone after it.

Once you truly understand that, the wonderful part is that you are in power. You can change everything. You do not have to live a mediocre life. If the life you have isn't a good life, you're not stuck with it. Whatever the circumstances you find yourself in, you can change them by changing the input you allow into your mind, by telling yourself new, powerful and uplifting stories. Is it work? Yes. Is it worth it? Only you can answer that. If it's worth it to you, I promise you that the principles in this book will help you get there.

6. Reframe

When the student is ready,
the teacher will appear—
the teacher has always been there.
Wayne Dyer

We've talked a lot in this book about your belief window and how it affects every aspect of your life. Let's say you've taken a good look at what's on your belief window—all those messages and experiences that have accumulated over the years—and you realize that it's not helping you succeed.

First of all, let me say good for you for taking that important step! It's not easy to admit that your own beliefs are getting in the way of your living the life you want. I know that it can be painful, and scary, and depressing, but I also know that it doesn't have to stay that way.

So now what? How can you change those old beliefs? How can you reroute those superhighways in your brain?

The rubber-band technique

What each of us needs to do with negative beliefs is reframe them. We need to find new ways to interpret all that information we've absorbed over the years. One of the best practical tools I know for starting that process—and it is a process—is the rubber band technique. I first learned this technique from Richard Burnett, one of my mentors in life and in business, and I've been sharing it ever since. It's unbelievably simple, but it's also extremely effective.

This is what you do. Find a rubber band, and put it around your wrist. Every time you find yourself doing negative self-talk: "Oh, I'm not very good at this ... I'll never pass that test ... I'll never build that business ... I've failed before and I'll fail again ... I'm overweight ... she (or he) will never go out with me ...." Anytime you hear that negative self-talk in your head, take that rubber band, pull it back, and snap it on your wrist.

I promise you that at the end of the day, two things are going to happen. First, your wrist is going to be a little sore. And second, you're going to have a startling realization about how much negative talk you really do tell yourself over the course of the day. If you do this for two, three, or four days a week, you're going to get better at it. You'll start avoiding that negative self-talk. You're going to want to make sure you don't have to keep snapping that rubber band, because your wrist is going to be sore.

In the last chapter we talked about Dr. Shad Helmstetter's concept of the superhighway in your brain. Helmstetter also talks about how important it is to override the negative superhighway. This rubber band technique is one way to start doing that.

Suppose you're a student coming up on a big test. You may be telling yourself that it's going to be too hard, or that you've never passed this type of test before. You snap that rubber band on your wrist when your self-talk starts, but instead of letting that negative message in, you reframe the thought and turn it into a positive message. You snap that rubber band and you tell yourself, "I am smart. I am capable of passing this test." Or you can say, "I am in the process of getting better at this. I am in the process of studying for this test which is going to allow me to pass it."

It works the same way in business. Maybe you're a salesperson, and you keep telling yourself that you're not good at making cold calls. You snap your rubber band, and you say to yourself, "I am good at cold-calling." Or you say, "I am in the process of becoming better at cold calling." Some people seem to find the "I am in the process of (fill in the blank)." formula more comfortable, but either will work.

If you'll do that on a regular basis for 90 days, you will begin to override that negative superhighway in your brain. All those neurons firing together on your negative path are going to start to firing on a positive path. You're going to begin replacing those negative messages on your belief window with positive ones. It is possible. It's been scientifically proven that it's possible. Does it take work? Yes. Is it worth it? Absolutely.

Just try it. Every time you start that negative self-talk—and boy, you'll find we are really good at talking negatively to ourselves—you snap that rubber band and immediately reframe it into a more positive message. Maybe one of your friends has just said something that hurt you. Instead of telling yourself that you're a terrible friend, you snap that rubber band and say, "I am in the process of becoming better at being a friend. I am in the process of understanding more about myself."

With 90 days of the rubber band technique, you can totally override that negative highway. Remember our example of being stuck in traffic? Once you've practiced reframing, the next time you find yourself in a traffic jam, you can find a positive outlook. Instead of all the negative thoughts that make being stuck in traffic even more miserable, you can say, "Wow, this gives me time to talk to my wife." Or, "This gives me time to listen to that audiobook I've got going." Or even just, "Look at the beautiful scenery." Life is so much better when you have that kind of an outlook. You'll find also that more and more people want to be around you.

I'm sure you've noticed when you're in that negative, foul mood how most people don't want to be around you—even your own family. Nobody likes to be in that environment. The good thing is you can change all of that. Your positive outlook can be a mental magnet to attract others to you. When I teach sales teams and ball players and people about this kind of positive energy—when I share that excitement and that hope—it's contagious. You can do the same. You can walk into a room full of strangers and you'll own that room.

When I'm working with the teenagers I mentor, I use the example of having to give a talk in class. I tell them that the minute they walk into that room and up to that podium, they can own that room. You can do the same. It's all due to the mental picture you carry inside yourself. If you walk into that room with your shoulders slumped and worried about it being a room full of your own classmates—or your co-workers, if it's a business presentation—it's going to be a disaster. It's a law. It can't be any other way.

On the other hand, if you walk into that room with your shoulders back, your head up high, and you've got that positive energy about you that says, "I own this. This is mine," then bingo! You've got it. It really does work that way.

Read, listen, study

There are other important tools for reframing negative messages and overriding the negative superhighway. Motivational books can be a great help. If you're really serious about turning your life around, you should be reading or listening to at least one motivational book a month. Some people say one per week. That may be too extreme, but I think most people can do one per month.

I have a particular formula for reading motivational books to help me get the most out of them. I read with two things in my hand: a yellow highlighter and a red ink pen. The first time I go through the book, I highlight it in yellow everything that jumps out at me as being significant. Then I go back through the book a second time, not reading the whole book, just the portions I've highlighted in yellow. From those, I pick out the ideas I consider really important and I underline them in red. Then I'll make notes in the margins and at the top and bottom of the page writing down how I feel about that and how I can apply it to my life. You may find another reading formula that works better for you, but the most important part, of course, is the last step: applying what you read. I can tell you it works. You may even become addicted to reading, and that's a good thing.

Let me give you an example. I mentioned earlier that when I took over the car rental agency, we had a staff meeting every Thursday night. At the meetings, I shared some of the business philosophy I had learned from W. Clement Stone and others, and we shared motivational books. Everybody was required to go out and buy a motivational book—some kind of positive, uplifting book. We reimbursed them. The company didn't have much money but I allotted it out of our small budget so that we could reimburse all of the employees, from the managers to the car washers. Each of them read a book. They had 30 days to finish their book, and when they finished, they had to write a book report and present it at the Thursday night meeting. That way we all got to learn. Even if we hadn't read the book ourselves, we all got to learn what the book was about. We learned what principles the reader had gleaned from it and how to use them. We did that for several years. Everybody on the staff was always reading positive, motivational books and doing book reports. Some people might say that was corny, but it worked. It absolutely worked. It was part of our success. We out-worked everybody, we out-believed everybody, and we also out-read everybody. It was fun, too. Some of these people were kind of shy when we first started working together, but you should have seen how excited they were to present their book reports in the meeting. It really was contagious.

Along with motivational books, take advantage of all the technology that's available today. You can find great motivational teachers on the internet. You can find motivational videos on YouTube; you can also find plenty of positive blogs and podcasts. A simple search will turn up all kinds of possibilities.

Make your car a library, especially when you're taking long trips. Instead of listening to music, plug in an audiobook. Put in a disc with uplifting messages that you can listen to. Turn your car radio into a library of success.

If you live near a big city, you may have the chance to hear some of the great motivational speakers in person. Take advantage of the opportunity—and take a notebook with you! It's important to keep adding positive input; after all, that negative highway and negative belief window have probably existed in your life for years.

Create a positive environment

Another important part of reframing is creating a positive, affirming environment around you. Consider looking into local chapters of organizations like Toastmasters or the Optimist Club. Both of those are wonderful organizations that will keep adding positive input to your belief window. In these and similar clubs or organizations, you'll find yourself among like-minded people. Your environment and the people you surround yourself with all contribute to your belief window. Surround yourself with positive people.

The obvious question, of course, is what do you do when you find yourself in a negative environment? The best thing to do is to leave that environment, but that may not always be possible. If for some reason you can't leave, then you work on overriding the negative with the tools we've been describing. And as hard as it may be, sometimes you may have to give up a few friends who are just poison in your life. You can't afford the luxury of being around people who are so negative. They will drag you down.

You know what I'm talking about. If you're a sports fan like me, for example, you can name many talented teams that have been beaten not by their opponents on the field or on the court, but by dissension among themselves. I saw it happen plenty of times when I was coaching. It was the same thing with the car rental agency; one of the reasons we went through 93 people in the first year was that there were some people who couldn't, or wouldn't, be part of a positive team effort.

Let me be clear: I never give up on people, but you will do them a better service by putting them to the side, at least for a while, and keeping on your own path. If you stay on your own positive, uplifting motivational path, one day they may be able to look at you and say, "Hmmm, maybe I need to make a change. If he or she can do it, then so can I." You can never give up on people.

Forgiving the past

There's one more essential element of reframing your beliefs and creating a positive environment. It's forgiveness. The best example of forgiveness I've ever seen was my own mom. She was a wonderful, loving lady who went through some very hard times in her life. She went through a painful divorce, and afterward had a lot of struggles to earn enough just to feed her family, let alone make her house payment and car payment. She had a tough time, but eventually she found a way to let go of any baggage of hurt and bitterness. I watched her let go of all that negative junk that keeps any of us from being the best that we can be. She learned the art of forgiveness and it totally turned her life around. The great, loving person that she had always been was again allowed to blossom. Even in her later years, when she was battling cancer, there was no bitterness. There was no "Why me?" or "This isn't fair." There was only love, and it made all the difference.

Letting go of hurt isn't easy. Forgiveness isn't easy. Reframing isn't easy. None of this work is. Changing your life is not for the faint of heart. But I guarantee that you will find it's worth it.

7. Invest in Yourself

Faith is taking the first step even when
you don't see the whole staircase.
Martin Luther King, Jr.

In the last chapter I mentioned my good friend Richard Burnett. In addition to being a mentor of mine, he is also a very successful businessman, and I want to tell a bit of his story.

Years ago, when he got started in the home-based business and network marketing arena, he did so by answering an ad in the paper, just as many people do. He discovered that the company required a large investment to get started. Richard didn't have the money. What he did have was a commitment and an understanding that sometimes opportunities come with a cost. Sometimes you have to pay a price for them. He went out and borrowed every dime he could. He tapped all of his friends and he finally came up with the money. He got involved in the company, and it became the beginning of a successful career. Today he's very well off financially and he helps a lot of people. He's a great guy. I often wonder, though, what would've happened if he had not invested in himself back then. Where would he be today if he had not gone out to borrow and scrape together all the money it took to get involved with that particular company? That decision opened up a career for him that has lasted for decades.

My wife and I had a similar experience. Many years ago, we opened up a juice bar inside a Family Fitness Center. Before we ever even got the doors open, we had to invest about $10,000. We had to have all the licenses and the permits, and because we were dealing in health foods and drinks, we had to have special plumbing, ice machines, refrigerators and all sorts of things. It was endless. But that was what it would take to open this business, and I understood the basic law of business: It takes money to make money. It didn't stop there, either. Every day we were open, either Cindy or I would go to the store and spend, at bare minimum, $100 a day buying more bananas, more strawberries, more peaches, more produce to make healthy salads, more cups, more everything. It was incredible. But again, I understood that was part of doing business.

Why am I telling you these stories? Look again at the title of this chapter: **Invest in Yourself.** So far in this book, you've learned about examining your belief window, about improving the input you receive, and about reframing your self-talk. Putting all of those things together, and taking control of your life, also means being willing to invest in yourself.

I'm not just talking about money. Yes, that's one way to invest, and it can be important, but it's not the only investment you need to make.

Invest your time

You need to be willing to invest your time. Lasting change doesn't happen overnight. It takes time and patience. Remember our rubber-band technique for reframing? It takes a good 90 days to reprogram those neurons and reroute that negative superhighway. Those negative messages on your belief window accumulated over a number of years. They won't be replaced in an instant. They can and will be replaced if you invest the time to do it.

But time alone won't do it either. You can't just sit and wait. You also need to invest in practice. That means practicing your rubber-band technique, practicing your reframing, practicing to improve whatever skills you are working to acquire. If you're a salesperson, maybe it means practicing your cold-call technique and sharpening your sales skills. If you're an athlete—or an aspiring athlete, like I was as a kid—you need to practice, and practice, and practice, to become the best you can be.

The point of all this investment is this: You can change your life.

You don't have to allow your past to mess up your future. You don't have to allow your old beliefs to condition your thinking and control your actions.

Don't be an elephant

Circuses and zoos have mostly stopped doing this—thank goodness!—but in the old days, they had a particular way of training elephants. They would take a baby elephant and put a big chain around one of its legs. They would attach the chain to a huge stake in the ground and no matter how hard that baby elephant tried, it couldn't pull the stake out of the ground. As the elephant grew older and bigger, it would become conditioned to stay put. A full-grown elephant, weighing tons, could easily pull that stake out of the ground, but when they put that chain around its leg and attached it to something, the adult elephant wouldn't even attempt to move because it had been conditioned by its past experiences. How many times in life do we find ourselves doing the same thing?

We let our past experiences condition us. We tell ourselves, "I failed at a business 20 years ago," or "I failed in a marriage 10 years ago," or "I failed at my last relationship two months ago" and we let that influence all of the decisions that we make about a business or a marriage or a relationship. It would be much better for us to examine why we failed at the business, why our marriage failed, or what happened to that last relationship. Too often we don't do that because it's too painful. Instead, we just decide that we'll never again attempt to do a business or a marriage or a relationship. That's just sad. Wouldn't it be better to invest the time and the effort to examine your past mistakes and learn from them?

Then the next time you start a business, or a relationship, or a marriage, or you go back to school, or whatever your situation, you're going to be much better off because you've had experience and will be much wiser for it.

Leave your baggage

You can—and should—learn from your past, but you take those lessons and invest in yourself to move forward with them. We've all got to learn from the past; if we don't, well, that old saying about history repeating itself is true. We can't let the past bury us either. Too many people carry so much baggage from their past that they're not able to move forward. Have you ever seen people staggering through an airport, loaded down with bags? I'm always fascinated watching them, and I can't help thinking, do they really need all of those suitcases for this trip? Let go of that heavy baggage that you're carrying around. It does nothing for your future. It just weighs you down and drags you down. Learn to leave the suitcases full of junk behind you. That's something else that will take time and practice, but I promise you it will be worth it.

Aren't you worth it? Isn't achieving the life you want worth it? In business we talk about ROI, <u>R</u>eturn <u>o</u>n <u>I</u>nvestment. Let me tell you, the ROI on investing in yourself is huge. It's the best investment you can make.

As I said earlier, you may need to invest some money. Maybe it's for training, or going back to school, or for buying motivational books. Maybe you're considering a home-based business. That will most likely require some investment of money, maybe a substantial amount, but again, all of these things are investments in yourself, and the dividends are priceless.

Remember that all of this is your choice. Every principle I'm sharing in this book is something I've learned through experience, but applying any of them is your choice. You can choose to deny them and go on about your life, or you might say, "Wow, let's give this a shot. Let's see about changing some of the things in my life that I'm not happy with." I promise you, if you'll put these principles to the test, you'll be amazed at how well they work.

Everything is possible to those who believe and are willing to roll up their sleeves and do the work. I often tell people to get up off the couch, turn the TV off, and get back into the game of life. It is a matter of choice. How badly do you want whatever it is you say you want? Only you can decide that. We all have failures in life. The winners—the ones that you read about, the ones who have the great successes—are always the ones who got up off the floor, dusted themselves off, and got back in the game.

Investing in others

You may even find that investing in yourself makes it possible for you to invest in others. You may be able to help other people who are struggling because of what you have learned from your experiences. You can say, "I have felt the way you do, but here's what I found." You can make a difference not only in your own life, but in the lives of others.

Earlier I told you about my wife Cindy going back to school. She made an enormous investment of time and effort to do that. It wasn't easy for her or for our family, but the return on that investment goes on and on. Her investing in herself has benefited not only our family, but also all of the students she teaches. Every day she makes a difference in their lives. We've seen the results over and over again.

Just today, as I'm writing this, I had a phone call from a young man who was in her class for two years. I had the privilege of mentoring him. We made a difference in his life. Now he's back in North Carolina. He stays in touch with us, and now he's out there making a difference in other people's lives using what he learned in Cindy's class.

When you invest in yourself, the rewards can be beyond anything you can imagine. But this is also true: If you don't invest in yourself and your dream, then it's nothing but a mere wish.

A man and a mouse

Another one of my heroes is Walt Disney. Think about the amazing legacy he left behind him: all of those wonderful films he produced, all of the amazing characters he created, and all the marvelous theme parks he conceived.

I love Walt Disney, and I love Disneyland, but Disneyland was not created by a wish. It was created by a man who had a dream. He was rejected many times, but he refused to give up. Legend has it that he was actually fired from a newspaper job for a lack of imagination and creativity. Just think about that for a moment. We've already talked about belief windows. What might have gone on Walt Disney's belief window after being fired for not being creative enough? He could have said, "I'm not good in this area. I don't have any creativity. I better settle for something else even though it's not my dream."

But Walt Disney had a choice, just as we all do. He chose not to settle for less than his dream. Instead he rolled up his sleeves and went to work. What he put on his belief window was, "Well, I'll show you." Then he went out there and showed the world.

Here in my office and on my desk, I have many of Walt Disney's sayings. I quote him often. Right now I'm looking at one of my favorites. It says, "It's kind of fun to do the impossible." That's what Walt Disney did. He created the impossible. He also said, "When you believe in something, believe in it all the way."

I live by those messages. They work. They're true. Several years ago, we had a family reunion at Disneyland with all of my kids and their spouses and all of our grandkids. We spent a couple of days there, not only enjoying the family, but also enjoying the magical atmosphere of Disneyland. When you walk through those gates, you can feel it in the air. What is it? It's energy, it's optimism, it's hope. It's the feeling that all things are possible.

You and I can create those same environments within our homes, within our families, within our businesses, and within our lives. Just use Walt Disney's example. Here's one last Disney story: During our family reunion at Disneyland, I saw something that literally brought tears to my eyes. It was a statue of Walt Disney, standing there like he's looking out over the kingdom that he created. His right hand is stretched out. His left hand is down, holding the hand of Mickey Mouse.

When I saw that statue, it brought out the coach in me. It brought out the ballplayer in me. It brought out the dreamer in me. Look what they've created. Walt Disney once said, "Remember it all started with a mouse." And here was this statue of Walt hand-in-hand with Mickey

Mouse overlooking Disneyland, looking out over everything they had created, the joy that they have created in millions and millions of families' lives. We had our entire family stand underneath the statue and take a family picture that now hangs in my office.

What I'm telling you with this book is that you and I can do that very same thing. It all starts not with a mouse, but with a crusade. It all starts with your dream, and your belief in whatever it is that you want to do to make a difference. Not a day goes by that I don't look for avenues to make a difference in somebody's life. What I love about the home-based business arena, where I have chosen to work for 30+ years, is that I don't get paid unless I'm making a difference in people's lives. I think that's wonderful.

That investment you make in yourself and in your dream can become an investment in others, in making a difference in people's lives. It's an investment in making the world a better place, and that's a wonderful thing.

The next time you go to Disneyland, look for that statue of Walt Disney and Mickey Mouse. You'll see what I mean.

8. Your Gift to the World

*If we all did the things we are
capable of doing, we would
literally astound ourselves.*
Thomas Alva Edison

There's something you should know about me. I still have a lot of little kid in me. I think all dreamers should have a little kid in them. On my desk I have a picture of Peter Pan and Tinkerbell flying through the air with the three kids. The caption underneath it says, "Grow wise, grow strong, but never grow up."

Sometimes, to be a dreamer, you've got to have some of that little kid in you. Remember the little kid you used to be? The one who thought that everything was possible? The one who thought that when you grew up, you could be whatever you wanted to be? That's the little kid we're talking about.

That little kid always got excited about Christmas. For me, it was always a favorite time. It still is. My wife will tell you that I can get excited about Christmas in July, as soon as I start to see some Christmas decorations. I love Christmas time. Why? First of all, it brings out a lot of that little kid in me, but just as importantly, there's a special feeling in the air around Christmas time. Everything and everyone seems more loving and compassionate. For me as a believer, it's also the joy of celebrating the birth of Jesus Christ. I'm old-school; I don't say happy holidays. I say Merry Christmas.

Of course I remember when I was a little kid, going to bed on Christmas Eve and being all excited, waiting for Santa Claus to come. Sometimes my sister and I would even sneak out in the middle of the night to peek, even though we weren't supposed to get up until the next morning. We could see the Christmas tree and all the presents underneath it. My grandmother really prided herself on Christmas bows, and she made beautiful bows to put on all the gifts. When we'd get up on Christmas morning, we would see all these wonderful packages wrapped in pretty paper with her handmade bows on them.

Here's a question for you: as beautiful as each of these gift packages may be, what is its real value? You don't really know what the value is until you take the bow off, unwrap the package, open the box and see what's inside. As long as that gift sits under the tree in its wrapping paper, it remains just a pretty package. Once you open it and take the gift out, you get to use that gift. That's where the value is. That's where the excitement is, in putting that gift to use.

You and I each have gifts to give to the world. I firmly believe that the good Lord up above has blessed each of us with different abilities and gifts and talents. Our gifts are definitely not the same. When I was a little kid, I wanted to grow up to be a country western singer, but I didn't have the talent for that. I marvel at other people who have that musical talent and ability. Did they have to work on it and develop it? Of course they did. For me, I had to accept that I didn't have the gift of music, so I was never going to be a country singer. What I did do is develop the gifts that I was given. I learned that part of my gift is teaching and making a difference in people's lives.

If each and every one of us has our own gifts and talents, what do we do with them? I believe the Lord has given us these gifts for a purpose, and I believe that purpose is to make a difference on this earth while we are here. I believe our ultimate purpose is to help others.

Finding your gifts

You might ask, "Barry, how do I know what my gift is?" My answer is another question: Where is your passion? That's the biggest clue to uncovering your gift. What gets you excited? What gives you goosebumps on the back of your neck? Most often, that's where you'll find your gift.

Ask other people. This is a great way to discover your gifts, maybe some you didn't realize you have. If you have the courage to do it, ask your family and friends what they think your gifts and talents are. They'll tell you. For some people, it's an ability to communicate. For others, it's athletics, or science, or music, or math.

Your life experiences can help you identify your gifts. That's how I discovered some of my own gifts. Remember, I was that kid always picked last in PE, and I was the kid who got put into the game when it was already lost. I worked hard to turn that around, to turn myself into a good player, and that experience taught me that I have a gift for determination and hard work.

As I got older and had the opportunity to become a coach myself, I realized that experience also helped me discover my gift for coaching. I was determined that none of my players would suffer the pain and embarrassment that I had felt. I was passionate about that—remember, your passions will help you find your gifts—and so I was determined to ensure that every player on my team felt important. I worked to build their self-esteem as well as their playing skills, and I learned in the process that I had a gift for coaching.

The point is, we've all got our own talents. Once you discover those talents—and chances are you already know what talents you have—then, as Stephen Covey says, "You need to sharpen the saw." You need to develop your talents and abilities and continue to improve on them. Why? First, of course, improving your abilities makes you better able to support yourself and your family. But that's not all. The more you develop your talents, the more people you can help and the more you can make a difference in the world.

Our world needs help. Whatever your beliefs, I think that you and I can all agree on that. I want you to think about this: Your gift might just be the one that makes all the difference out there in the world. For sure, it'll make a difference in your own world—in your own immediate circle—but you never know how many lives you're going to touch when you have developed that gift or that special talent that you have.

There's a Chinese proverb somewhere that says "Happy is he who teaches." My wife and I both have a love of teaching, and it's a gift I think we share. We love teaching these principles for success, and even more importantly, we both love to see the twinkle in somebody's eye when they get it. That's when we know we've made a difference in that person's life. We know that they're going to go out and dust off their dreams and go conquer the world. It's an exhilarating feeling to do that for people.

It's never too late

Sometimes you find your gifts early in life; sometimes later. But whenever you find them, you can go on to keep developing your gifts throughout your life. You may even find new gifts much later in life. Sometimes you find yourself in a new arena and you start to realize that you have an aptitude for it. You have a gift that you didn't know you had, and it becomes another gift that you can develop and use. You are never too young—and you're never too old!—to discover more gifts and talents that you've been given.

What's even more exciting about all this is that we can put our gifts together to make an even bigger difference in the world. When I'm building a business team, I often tell people, "You bring your gifts and talents to the table, and I'll put my gifts and talents on the table, and we will not only learn from each other, but we'll make a smorgasbord here for the people joining our crusade."

We learn from each other. When we communicate openly, with no egos involved, when we put all our gifts together, there's no limit to what we can accomplish. We can make such a difference in our own communities and in that world that so needs our help.

What gift will **you** bring to the world?

9. How You See Yourself Matters Most

Someone's opinion of you
does not have to become your reality.
Les Brown

As you begin to practice the things we're talking about in this book, you will find that you begin to think differently about yourself. You will have started to clean off your belief window and you're doing more positive self-talk. You're reading your motivational books. You're working on developing your gifts. And as you do all those things, one day you're going to look in the mirror and realize that you are not seeing that same old self anymore.

There's a picture I keep on my desk. It's been around for a long time; you may have seen it. It's a photo of a little orange kitten looking in a mirror. The reflection the kitten sees in the mirror is a big, fierce lion. I love that image. I keep it nearby to remind me that how you see yourself matters.

Why is that important? It's important because the way you see yourself is exactly how the world will see you. And it's exactly how the world will treat you.

When we look in the mirror, we look at it through our belief window, and if that window is full of negative messages, we can't see ourselves clearly. It's becomes too easy to look in the mirror and see the worst. It's easy to fall into what I call "woe is me" syndrome. Then it spirals down to, "Woe is me, woe is the world, woe is the economy, woe is my job, woe is …" We go on and on. How often can we beat ourselves up? Too many of us beat ourselves up continually—and unnecessarily. We need to banish that "woe is me" outlook.

I once saw a quote that said "Argue for your limitations and, sure enough, they're yours." They're yours because your RAS will make them yours. So let's stop arguing for our limitations. We need to stop beating up on ourselves. Let's start arguing instead for our talents and our gifts and our passions.

Whom do you see in the mirror?

Be like the kitten. That tiny kitten looks in the mirror and sees a powerful lion. We look at that picture and we see the kitten's image of itself. If you look in the mirror and see a loser, or someone who is down and out, that's the image others will see of you. That's what's on your belief window and that's what people will see. If you see yourself as a winner who is living life to its fullest, other people will see that, too.

People will respond to your body language and what it says about how you see yourself. When you stand up straight and hold your head high, when your shoulders are back and you project optimism, people will respond to that. When you're talking on the phone, people will hear the energy and the passion in your voice, and they will respond accordingly. I can assure you that there is not enough of that energy in the world today, and I promise that when people see that energy in you or hear it in you they will be attracted to you. You'll be amazed at the people who will come into your life.

What I want you to see when you look in the mirror is the magnificent individual that you really are. If you are a believer, like me, you can think of this as seeing yourself the way God sees you. I believe God knows us better than we know ourselves, sees us with all the gifts we have been given, and wants the best for each of us.

When you look in that mirror I want you to see a powerful, gifted individual. I want you to see your inner lion. I want you to see someone who can create magic out there. I want you to see someone who is taking their gifts and using them to make a difference in the world. And guess what? You'll find that people are eager to join you in doing that.

Quantum energy

What accounts for that attraction? We've already talked about the law of attraction that says positive energy attracts positive energy, and we've talked about the RAS—the reticular activating system—that filters your outer world to match your inner world. There's also another theory that comes from the science of quantum physics. It's the idea of quantum energy, that everything in the universe is energy. That's another way of looking at what we have been talking about throughout this book: that your energy goes out into the universe and that same energy comes back to you. Quantum energy is the vibrational energy that we all give out. People are attracted to positive energy because there is not enough of it in their lives or in the world.

I experienced that myself back when I was working in that job that made me so miserable. I was looking for ways to improve my life, so I started going to a weekly presentation by the Success Motivation Institute. They were selling a self-improvement program that was way out of my reach financially at the time, but I kept going back every week because it felt like a refuge. I wanted to be around those like-minded, positive people who were delivering a positive, uplifting message.

People want to belong to something that's bigger than they are: a cause, a crusade, or an opportunity to make a difference in somebody's life. That's huge. People want it because there's not enough of it out there. In a previous chapter I mentioned organizations like the Optimist Club or the Toastmasters. They're gaining new members all the time. Why is that? It's because once people step into that positive, uplifting environment they want more of it.

When you are on a mission to make a difference—and I believe that we all should be on that mission in our own way, whatever that means to you—I promise that you'll find people will cross your path in the most unexpected ways.

There are no accidents

I also believe, and have taught for years, that in every situation you encounter, you can be assured that God is working behind the scenes.

Whenever we come across someone who needs help, it's rarely at a convenient time. It's always when you're in a rush to get somewhere or you've got to get home to cook dinner, or you've got a big test tomorrow, or you're late for a meeting, and all of a sudden somebody appears who needs help now. I don't believe that it's an accident or a coincidence. I believe that God—or your higher power, or the universe, however you understand that—has put that person in your path at that particular moment because you have a role to play in that situation. You are the one to make a difference in that person's life. It may be a small difference, or it may be a big difference, but that particular difference is one only you can make. The tragedy is how often we just ignore that situation and keep right on going. How often do we think, "Oh, I should, but I just don't have the time."? Or, "Oh, I should, but I just don't have a couple of extra dollars."? Or, "Oh, I should … I should … but … but … but …"?

This is also part of how you see yourself. If you take the time to realize it's not an accident that this person has been placed in your path right now, you can choose to make a difference. It is always your choice, but think about it. If you see yourself as the capable person you are, with all your God-given gifts and talents, you will see that you have what it takes to make a difference in that person's life. When you begin to think that way, you'll be amazed at how many people you can help during the course of a day, a week, a month … a lifetime.

Everybody has a story. The work that we are doing in this book will help you to understand your own story and to see yourself differently. When we do that, we begin to see others differently as well. If we truly want to make a difference in the world, we have an obligation: Whenever we come across a person, we should always leave their story better than how we found it.

When we begin to see every person we meet as someone with a unique story, we will begin to treat each other better. We won't be so tempted toward bad-mouthing them, or spreading gossip, or whispering behind their back, or bullying them. You can't know someone's burdens unless you've walked in their shoes. Don't add to their burden. There's plenty of meanness and unkindness out there; let's be kind to each other instead.

You may remember that I told you in the introduction to this book that I'm a maniac on a mission. That's how I see myself, and that mission is to put hope back into people's lives.

What do **you** see when you look in the mirror?

10. Facing Impossible Odds

Success is not final, failure
is not fatal: it is the courage
to continue that counts.
Attributed to Winston Churchill

When you're doing the hard work of changing your life and working toward your dream, there will be times when it seems like that dream is unreachable. You may feel that the odds are stacked against your success. I know that feeling well. I've had that feeling many times in my own life. When I get that feeling, I turn to some of my heroes for inspiration, and I want to introduce you to a couple of those heroes.

One of my all-time favorite heroes is Winston Churchill. I have read many books on Churchill and consider him one of the greatest figures of the 20th century. Unfortunately his story doesn't seem to be taught in school anymore; most of the teenagers I mentor tell me they've never heard of him. I think that's sad. There's so much we can learn from Churchill's example.

Churchill: leader and statesman

As a young man, Winston Churchill was a soldier who saw action in many different parts of the world, including service in World War I. He was first elected to Parliament in 1900, at the age of 25, and went on to hold many different positions in the government. Although he had his successes and failures over the years politically, and was often seen as controversial, he became a great statesman. In the 1930s, as Hitler's power was growing and he was arming Germany, Churchill warned Parliament and the British people that they needed to prepare for war. He was convinced that Hitler would eventually attack, but no one wanted to hear his warnings. He was even booed in Parliament when he tried to persuade the members that Germany and Hitler were becoming dangerous and that Britain should build up its own military. Meanwhile Germany got stronger, their air force got bigger, their army got bigger, and Hitler kept moving forward. Churchill was like a voice crying in the wilderness telling the British people that we've got to get ready because there's a fight coming.

The Prime Minister in those years was Neville Chamberlain. He knew that Britain was unprepared to go to war, and he wanted to find a way to avoid conflict with Germany. In September 1938 Chamberlain met with Hitler, and along with the French prime minister, signed an agreement that was supposed to prevent Hitler from taking any more countries.

When Chamberlain came back to England, he got off the plane waving the signed document, which was called the Munich Agreement. Churchill didn't believe the agreement was worth the paper it was written on. In Parliament, he said, "Britain and France had to choose between war and dishonor. They chose dishonor. They will have war." Needless to say, Hitler ignored the Munich Agreement and continued to take more territory. The following year he invaded Poland and as Churchill had predicted, Britain got drawn into the war. Not long afterward, Chamberlain had to resign when it became clear he didn't have the support of the people anymore. In May 1940, Churchill was appointed the new prime minister.

It was a dark time. England was unprepared and by then, Germany had the greatest Air Force the world had ever seen. The Nazis had taken over all of Europe, including France.

When France surrendered, Churchill said that Britain would fight on alone. One of the French generals said, "In three weeks England will have her neck wrung like a chicken." Remember that part.

Hitler knew he could not take England without controlling the air first. So here came the Luftwaffe, the German air force, at the time the greatest air power the world had ever seen. Hitler's troops were in France waiting to cross the English Channel to invade England but first they had to control the air. That was how the Battle of Britain came about: the conflict between the Luftwaffe and the British Royal Air Force (RAF).

Many years ago, my wife gave me a big picture for Christmas. It shows a British Spitfire—that's what the RAF flew—soaring through the air. Every time I look at that picture, it reminds me that impossible odds can be overcome. The German air marshal, Hermann Göring, had promised Hitler that it would only take days for his Luftwaffe to destroy the RAF. But the days turned into weeks and the weeks turned into months and the Battle of Britain continued to rage every day. Where was Churchill? He wasn't in some bomb shelter behind the lines protecting himself. Every day he was out among the people, reassuring them and cheering them on. Every night he was on the radio giving some of the most profound speeches the world had ever heard. Winston Churchill encouraged the people to fight on, to keep going, and to not give up. He put every fiber of his being into defeating Hitler.

The Battle of Britain lasted from July to October 1940. Hitler finally realized that he couldn't take England and turned his attention toward Russia instead. Churchill, knowing what the French generals had said about England getting its neck wrung, said, "Some neck, some chicken."

Winston Churchill stood up to Hitler when no one else would. As a student of history, I believe that if it hadn't been for Churchill standing up to Hitler—if Hitler had been able to take England—the United States would have had a much more difficult job stopping Germany. The British pilots and the British people took horrible losses every day and every night with the constant bombings. But they would not quit and Churchill was the reason. He picked the nation up by its boot straps and carried it. It's a great lesson for all of us. Study Winston Churchill. Study the impossible odds that he took on; study the disappointment he had when he attempted for years to warn the people what was about to happen. They wouldn't listen to him. They booed him, they hissed him, and they said he was crazy.

Churchill's story reminds me of the Bible story of Noah and the ark. When Noah was building that ark, all the neighbors laughed at him. They told him he was crazy but as I understand the story, when the floods came and the ark was floating off, there were still people trying to get on board.

There's a lesson for all of us in Churchill's story and in Noah's story: Never underestimate your vision or your belief in what you're doing.

Satchel Paige: mind over matter

I love to read history, and I find inspiration from Churchill and other historical figures, but my heroes come from other areas as well.

Another of my heroes is the great baseball pitcher Satchel Paige. Unless you're a die-hard baseball fan, you may not have heard of him. My favorite quote of his is this: "Never let the odds keep you from pursuing what you know in your heart you were meant to do."

Who was Satchel Paige? He was a pitcher in the old Negro leagues. In those days of the '20s, '30s and '40s, Negroes were not allowed to play in the major leagues. Satchel Paige became a legend in Negro Leagues because of his tremendous talent and pitching abilities. After Jackie Robinson finally broke the color barrier, becoming the first African-American player in the major leagues, Satchel Paige finally got his chance. Bill Veeck, the owner of the Cleveland Indians, was quite a showman. He brought Paige up from the Negro Leagues and into the majors in 1948.

No one really knows how old he was when he finally made it to the majors, because Satchel Paige didn't allow anybody to know how old he really was. When anyone asked, he told them, "Age is a question of mind over matter. If you don't mind, it doesn't matter." It's estimated that he was born around 1906, so when he finally made it to the majors he was in his 40s. Think about that: After decades of success in the Negro Leagues, he finally got to the majors in his 40s. That's when big league players are normally retiring. In 1948, Satchel Paige helped the Cleveland Indians win the World Series—as the oldest rookie ever in the major leagues. He retired in 1953, estimated to be in his late 40s at the time. He might have been much older than that.

Now here's the even more amazing part of the story. Twelve years later the owner of the Kansas City A's, Charlie Finley, who was a bit of a maverick, signed Satchel Paige as a publicity stunt for the last few weeks of the season. The team wasn't going anywhere, and Finley was looking to attract some fans to the games. He put Satchel Paige out in the bullpen with a rocking chair. Everybody came to see this great legend, and in the last week of the season, Charlie Finley let Satchel Paige go into a major league game and pitch again. How old was he at the time? He was probably at least 58, maybe much older. Satchel Paige pitched three shutout innings that day. It's one of the most amazing stories you will ever hear in sports. It says a lot about old age and about what you can and can't do.

Satchel Paige pitched against big league players who were less than half his age and he pitched three shutout innings. So don't let anyone tell you that you're too old to change, or that you're too old to follow your dream, or that you're too old to do anything. That's bull. You're never too old. When you think you are, think of Satchel Paige. He used to say, "Don't look back because something might be gaining on you." He never looked at his age and neither should you or I.

It may not seem that Satchel Paige and Winston Churchill had much in common. But I think they both demonstrate what we've been talking about all through this book: that nothing is impossible to those who believe.

Both of these men faced seemingly impossible odds and refused to be discouraged by them. Both of them had years of struggles and failures. Failure doesn't have to matter. Past failure doesn't mean that you will fail in the future; it just means that you have experience to draw upon and learn from.

Both of these heroes are examples of what can happen when you believe and you're not afraid to roll up your sleeves and go to work. If they could achieve what they did, despite the odds against them, what might you be able to achieve?

11. The Power of Positive Influence

Life is an exciting business, and most
exciting when it is lived for others.
Helen Keller

In the last chapter, I told you about a couple of my personal heroes. Those are just two of the many people, near and far, who have been a positive influence in my life. I want to challenge you here to look back and think about that. Who has most influenced your life?

Maybe it was someone in your immediate family. For many people, it's their mom or dad, or maybe a brother or sister. For others, it's a teacher, or a coach, or a pastor. Maybe you have a friend who has been your most positive influence. I can almost guarantee that if you think back, you can identify someone who has influenced you for good. Maybe you have been fortunate enough to have many people who have affected you, or changed you, or inspired you. If that's the case, good for you! Be thankful for that.

Maybe you haven't been that fortunate. Maybe you've had a tougher life, and you have to search your memory for that person or persons.

When you identify that person, picture them in your mind. If you have an actual picture of that person handy, stop and take a good look at it. Take some time to remember how that person made you feel. Maybe it was just someone who cared enough to teach you, or to help you with a math problem, or to stick up for you at school when you were being bullied. Maybe it was a coach who saw more in your ability than you saw in yourself. Remember the difference that person made in your life. Think about how grateful you were for him or her.

Now consider this: You can be that person for someone else. In fact, you can be that person for lots of people. You can be that positive influence for them. Wouldn't that be a wonderful thing to do?

Years ago, when I was winning all those baseball championships, I saw the movie "Patton," starring George C. Scott. It's an old movie now, but I was so fascinated then by Patton's story and his leadership that I actually went to the movie theater a dozen different times, paid money every time, and watched the movie again. It had a profound effect on me because it was about leadership, about being out in front, and not giving orders from way behind the lines.

I believe that each of us has leadership ability within us, and we have a responsibility to take time to develop that ability for the betterment of humankind. It's a constant study. You learn as you go, but it is an ongoing study. It is self-development. Each of us carries the ability within us, but we have to put in the work to make it better and to make us better.

I'm not one for foul language, but over the years I've come to the conclusion that there are two types of leaders out there. The first type of leader is someone you would follow to hell and back. The second type? That's the one you just tell to go to hell.

Of course, we all want to become that first type of leader, right? That's the one who does the right thing for everyone. How do we do that? We do that by being the leader who is not on an ego trip. We do that by being the leader who really gets down in the trenches with people, and works with them, and helps them. Whatever the situation, we want to lighten their load.

Seize the moment

When you work at becoming that type of leader, you will be surprised by what happens. You never know when it will come—maybe when you are in the midst of helping someone else, or developing your leadership skills—but you will have what I call an "Aha!" moment. It's a defining moment. It may be a sudden revelation or a key realization. I guarantee you that it will come; please don't be so busy that you miss it. When you recognize that moment, take the time to analyze it. Grasp it, write it down, carry it with you, and look at it on a regular basis. Those moments are precious, not only to us in our own lives, but also to the people that we can influence because of that moment or that revelation.

Wayne Dyer describes that moment as *satori*. Satori is a Buddhist term that means "sudden enlightenment" or "instant awakening." It's the moment when, all of a sudden, you get it. All of a sudden, it's clear as a bell. It makes total sense to you. There's nothing more gratifying to a coach, or a mentor, or a person who just wants to make a difference in somebody's life, when you see that happen. You see that your student gets it: Their eyes light up, and you can see them realizing, "Wow, look what I can do!" We've all heard the saying, "When the student is ready, the teacher will appear." The other part of that saying is, ". . . and the teacher was always there, just waiting for us to be ready to take the next step."

Fire walking

One of my own *satori* moments happened at a leadership school here in Las Vegas called Rapport Leadership International. The school was originated by Mike and JoAnn Knapp, based on teachings from an exclusive leadership school in Japan. I have great respect for those two and what they taught me within that company, within that organization and those classes.

I was part of the sales team for the school, and of course each salesperson was required to take the classes so we knew what we were selling. These were three-day classes—

36 hours of concentrated training—and they were intense. In fact, in my first class, I hadn't been sitting there more than three minutes before I was thinking, oh, Barry, what have you done to yourself? But by the time the class was over, three days later, it was remarkable to see the change in the people who took the class.

All of a sudden, these people had a fire within them. There was nothing they couldn't accomplish. They had been doing the kind of work that we have been talking about in this book, discarding their old baggage and replacing it with new, better thinking. One of the things the school taught was a fire walk class. I had seen Tony Robbins and several others on TV doing the fire walk—where people walk across hot coals or walk across broken glass and nothing happens to their feet—and I had always believed that there was a trick to it. But the night that I took that fire walk class at Rapport, I learned just how powerful the human brain is.

I did it. I literally walked across red hot coals and did not burn the bottom of my feet. You're probably asking, why on earth would anyone do that? The purpose of the fire walk is to show you what you are capable of. At the end, you're told, "If you can walk across hot coals like this and not burn your feet, what in life can't you do?" It takes extreme concentration to do the fire walk. The instructor, Mike Knapp, could look in your eyes and tell if you were ready. If he didn't think you were, you'd go to the back of the line and readjust your focus until you were ready to walk across those coals.

I can tell you from personal experience that there was no trick to it. There were no special fireproof slippers like I thought there might be. There was no Photoshopping; it was real. The wonderful part of it—my Aha! moment—was learning that the teachers were right. If you can do that, if the mind is powerful enough to tell you, "We're going to walk on these burning hot coals, and we're not going to burn our feet," that's an amazing thing. That's how much power each of us has within us, and we can learn how to use that. I hope that this book will help you to do that.

YES Incorporated

One of the great privileges in my life is helping other people to discover and develop their own power. While it's true that you can do this work at any age, I'm especially excited when I can introduce these ideas to young people, so as to help them recognize their potential early in life. For the past three years, I've been a mentor for high school students through a program that my wife teaches, called YES Incorporated.

When Cindy first started teaching the program, I thought it was just a business class, but it turned out to be much more than that. I had no idea how different it was until I actually went to their graduation. At the end of the year, there is a graduation ceremony just for that particular class. When I sat in the audience, I was blown away by the talent and accomplishments of the students in that program. I heard so many of the parents around me saying, "Wow, I wish I could have had a class like this when I went to high school." That graduation was another one of those Aha! moments for me. I suddenly understood that it wasn't just a business class. This class was all about getting down in the trenches and making a difference in kids' lives. It puts into practice all the things we've been talking about in this book.

The YES Incorporated class is a combined business and English class. High school juniors and seniors take the class for two hours a day. Instead of reading classic novels, they read current documents and business books that will relate to their future and to their life today. YES stands for the **Y**oung, the **E**mpowered, and the **S**killed, and that's the goal of the class: to prepare these kids for their future so that by the time they leave, they will indeed be young, empowered, and skilled. Cindy and her teaching partner bring all kinds of different opportunities into the classroom. The class includes guest speakers from all different walks of life. It also offers job shadowing, mock job interviews, career planning, résumé building, and adult mentorships. It's been a real honor for me to be a mentor for the kids in this class.

The kids actually lead the class. They even have a Toastmasters International Gavel Club in the classroom. They participate in the Gavel Club every week. They give their speeches, they are evaluated by their peers, and they run the classroom in all respects.

I know I'm prejudiced because this is my wife's class, but she's the only one in the state of Nevada teaching this particular class, and the difference that it has made in students' lives is phenomenal. I've seen it firsthand.

As I mentioned, the program includes mentoring of students by adult volunteers, and I've been privileged to do that for three years. The kids that I have mentored have just been an absolute joy in my life. I have learned lots from them, as I believe they have learned from me.

Recently one of our past YES graduates, a young woman I had mentored, came to our house for dinner to give us an update on what's been going on in her life. She brought a couple of friends with her so we could meet them, since they will be going into the YES class next year. It was just a joyous occasion; we had so much fun being around these like-minded young adults sharing their experiences. We talked about a lot of the ideas I have been sharing with you in this book, and I told them about my fire walk. When I told them how much power the mind has and that they have that same ability, they were so focused on what I was saying. I could see they were just enthralled with the concept. I guess you could say that they had gotten a dose of *The Book of Barry*. The next day we heard from them and they said after they left our house, they'd spent another hour talking about everything that they had learned. One of them said that the evening had been like "a car wash to the soul."

Why am I sharing this story with you? I think it's a beautiful example of the way that positive influence spreads. The principles that I have been sharing with you in this book are principles that I have been teaching and living by for years. Cindy has been sharing that journey with me, and has been bringing these principles into her classroom, sharing them with her students. I know that she has been a positive influence in her students' lives; many of them stay in touch with us and tell us so. And one of the most gratifying developments for both of us has been watching these wonderful young people go on to share what they have learned. They will go on to do great things, and they will in turn be a positive influence for others.

You may never know the ripple effect of what you do to make a difference in even one person's life. Think about the difference we can make together!

12. Alice in Wonderland and the Cheshire Cat

All you need is the plan,
the road map, and the courage
to press on to your destination.
Earl Nightingale

Have you ever read Lewis Carroll's classic book, *Alice in Wonderland*? There's a scene in it that is one of my all-time favorites. Alice is wandering through Wonderland when she comes to a fork in the road, where there is a big tree. Alice looks up into the tree and sees a big cat, the Cheshire Cat. Not knowing what else to do, Alice asks the Cat which way she should go. The Cat replies, "That depends a good deal on where you want to get to." When Alice says she doesn't care, the Cat responds, "Then it doesn't matter which way you go."

Think about that. There's a powerful message in the cat's reply. Do you know where you want to go? Do you know what you want? When you walk into a restaurant and the waiter asks what you would like to order, would you say, "Well, I don't know …"? What about your job? What about your career? Do you know? Here's a big one: What about your relationship? What about the person you may be thinking about spending the rest of your life with? Would you want your Cheshire Cat to say, "Well, then any relationship will do"? Or, "Well, then any career will do."? Or even, "Anything on the menu will do"? Of course you

wouldn't.

Leaving your choices to chance doesn't usually work out for the best. You have to know where you want to go in life. There's a verse in the Bible that says without a vision the people will perish, and I believe that's true. You have to have a vision for your life. The challenge is that most people don't understand that they really do have choices about their life. They may have traveled so many roads, and had so many disappointments, that they've lost hope. They've lost any belief that they can have what they want. We all feel that way at times. Life can sometimes beat you up, and it can make you lose sight of your dreams. It can cause you to lose hope that things can be different.

What does your road look like today, as you're reading this book? Maybe you're on a great road. Maybe you're right on track. If you are, good for you! Take the tools I've offered in this book and use them to keep moving forward on that road.

Maybe you're not where thought you'd be at this stage of your life. Maybe you're not on the road you'd like to be traveling. The good news is that you don't have to stay there. You can make the choice to change roads. Does it take courage? Yes. Will it be worth it? That's for you to decide.

My own life is an example. When I'm giving a talk or a training in a room full of people, I always tell them that I've had more failures than all of them combined. That's the truth. I had many successes in the sports world, winning many championships, but it took me years to find that kind of success in the world of business.

Many of the people I work with now are in home-based businesses. I know how disheartening it can be to put your heart and soul into that and then suddenly have the company go out of business. I've been there. I was once with a company that went out of business two weeks before Christmas. I had worked my tail off for that company, and they owed me a big check. In fact, they owed me $20,000.

Cindy and I had just adopted three young kids, and we were counting on that money. But there we were two weeks before Christmas: no business, no check, and three young children to support. It was a devastating blow for our family.

We got through it by the goodness of God and the caring of other people. Through our church, on Christmas Eve, there were so many gifts stacked on our doorstep that they stretched clear out to our driveway. To this day I have never in my life seen such an outpouring of love and caring. It made a world of difference to me and Cindy and our three young children. We never did learn the names of those caring, generous people, but we do know that they were following the example that Jesus Christ set out for all of us: to love one another.

So I know what it's like to have to change course and find a new road. I've had so many failures in the business world that it used to be the family joke at every Thanksgiving dinner. Someone in the family would ask (in front of everyone, of course): "Well, Barry, what career do you have this year? Well, Barry, what company are you representing this year?" And everybody would get a chuckle out of it. I'd chuckle too, even though I was a little bit embarrassed because I had gone through so many companies looking for the right ones. In spite of that, though, the good news was that Barry kept looking. I didn't let that affect me. I didn't put those judgments on my belief window. I had a vision of what I wanted, and so I kept moving forward. Eventually I found not just one, but several right companies that have benefited me and Cindy and our family for years.

Another direction

I know about the heartache of having to start over, but I also know that you can't give up. Let me tell you about another of my heroes from history, General O.P Smith. He was a Marine Corps commander during the Korean War, commanding the 1st Marine Division. This division had pushed the North Koreans clear up close to the Chinese border. They were in an area called the Chosin Reservoir.

Although General Douglas MacArthur had assured President Harry Truman that the Chinese would not enter into the war, Chinese forces were getting ready to support the North Koreans. One night, the Chinese attacked with thousands of soldiers, trying to isolate the 1st Marine Division from the rest of the allied forces. The division was surrounded, a long way from their lines. They had to fight for every inch, from the mountain tops to the gullies, to get back to their lines. As the story goes, there happened to be a reporter with this division during the Battle of the Choisin Reservoir. He approached General Smith and said, "General, considering the proud tradition of the United States Marine Corps, how does it feel to be retreating?" O.P. Smith looked the reporter in the eye and said, "Retreat? Hell, we're advancing in another direction." They succeeded, by the way. They succeeded without leaving any of the dead or wounded behind, and without leaving behind a single piece of equipment that the Chinese could use.

According to legend, when they finally reached the rest of the troops days later, they marched into camp singing the Marine Corps hymn. What I love about that story is what it says about starting over. Whenever you have to start over in life, it's okay. It's not an embarrassment. The embarrassment is not **starting over**; it's **when you don't start over**. It's when you just lie down and quit. That's the embarrassment.

If you're reading this book, you've picked it up for a reason. There's a message in here for you and maybe this particular message is it: It's okay to start over. It's okay to change course. It's okay to choose a new road. What's important is that you know where you want to go. Defeat never has to have the last word; it's okay to "advance in a new direction."

I want to tell you about a friend of mine who did exactly that. She took control of her life and set off on a new road.

Changing course: Lori's story

I've known Lori Davis for years. She is a very special woman with a heart of gold, always willing to help anyone in need.

During the great recession that hit in 2008, Lori was caught in a bad place. Her husband's business came to an immediate halt. Their income was reduced by as much as 90 percent. Some months, they had no income at all. Obviously, they had to make some difficult decisions; they were close to losing their house.

Lori, who was a speech pathologist, could have gone back to work, but at the same time, there were some family challenges that made it important for her to stay close to home. Being a woman of faith, Lori prayed about what to do. She concluded that she needed to stay home to help her family, so she decided to go into a home-based business. Well, of course, it takes money to build a business, and during this whole time they were short of money. The bills were stacking up, and at the same time one of her children had developed a huge drug problem.

If you've ever had a family member struggle with drugs, you know how hard that is. It can make life pure hell, but you never give up on your kids, and Lori was determined not to give up on her son. At the same time, she was just as determined not to give up on the business she was building. If ever anyone had reason to use every excuse in the book, it was Lori. She could have used every single "Yeah, but …" that has ever been uttered by someone attempting to build a business. But Lori knew that her family's livelihood depended on her succeeding. She knew she couldn't afford excuses, so even while she was taking care of all her family responsibilities, she never let it stop her from building her network marketing business.

With the particular network marketing company Lori had chosen, there were many trainings that she needed to attend, and those cost money as well—not only for the training classes themselves, but also for the out-of-state travel to get to them. She never missed any of the trainings. She put money aside as she could, even putting off paying a few bills to get to those trainings. She knew that she needed to invest in herself and her business. Eventually the training and the investment began to pay off and she started to grow her business.

Today, Lori has an organization with almost 35,000 people on her team. She's no longer worried about her house payment. She's no longer worried about the car payment. Best of all, her son has been drug-free for several years now. I have so much admiration and respect and love for this woman. Lori Davis is a shining example to any of us of what you can do when you believe in yourself, you know where you want to go, and you are willing to roll up your sleeves to go to work.

The power of determination: Jeff and Angela's story

I don't know a better example of the power of hard work and determination than Jeff and Angela Boyle. Jeff was actually fired from a company that he himself had started. In the wake of a power struggle among stock holders and false rumors that were spread about him, Jeff lost his job and his company. Imagine trying to cope with that! But that wasn't all. Later, as he was rebuilding his life and his business, Jeff was run over by a car. The accident left him in serious medical condition, and again, he lost his business. Even though he used his savings to pay his employees, that wasn't enough and he had to start over yet again. But Jeff persevered. In the end, he not only overcame serious business disappointment and financial failures, he also recovered from more than $400,000 in debt. Together, Jeff and Angela have built a very successful home-based business which has recently allowed them to purchase their dream home. Even though it would have been much easier for them to give up after all those challenges, they refused to let defeat have the last word. Instead they found themselves a new road and committed wholeheartedly to it.

We started this chapter talking about the message of the Cheshire Cat: If you don't know where you want to go, it doesn't matter what road you take. But when you do know where you want to go, and you commit to that road, you can follow it to the life you really want.

So think about it. When the Cheshire Cat asks where you want to go, what will your answer be?

13. Never Give Up

Never give in, never give in, never, never,
never, never—in nothing, great or small,
large or petty—never give in except
to convictions of honour and good sense.
Winston Churchill

There's no better example of never giving up than Winston Churchill, a man who faced impossible odds and not only came through to victory, but brought a whole nation with him.

Why is this message so important? I can think of so many examples—and I'll bet you can, too—of people who have come so close to their goal and then given up just before they reach it. There are hundreds of stories about the person who was two steps from victory, or two steps from achievement, when they quit and gave up. To me, that is a tragedy.

Everyone faces obstacles and setbacks. Sometimes we even face crushing defeats. When that happens, we always have two choices. We can just roll over and play dead, wallowing in our misery, or we can get back up, dust ourselves off, and go at it again. We can take the lessons we've learned from the defeat with us into the next venture or the next attempt at success.

In my ball playing and coaching days, we used to talk about the "Big Mo." That's momentum, and in sports, in business, or in life itself, you never know just when Big Mo is going to turn the tide for you.

I've spent a lifetime studying success and successful people. I'm sure there's an exception somewhere, but in all of my study, I've never met anyone or read a book on anyone who had instant success. Those who win and those who achieve success are those who don't quit. They're the ones who keep moving forward. They learn from their mistakes, they learn from their defeats, and they move on.

Babe Ruth once said, "It's hard to beat a person who never gives up." That doesn't mean it will be easy. There will always be roadblocks along the way. I think of that as the universe testing your metal to see how badly you want to reach your goal. Once the universe knows that you're not going to quit—that you're going to keep going until you have reached your goal—all of a sudden, things start to happen. Good things start coming your way.

Remember that your reticular activating system makes sure that your outside world matches your inside. Once your inside world is full of resolve, and commitment, and passion, and energy, then all of a sudden, that's exactly what your outside world is going to start to look like.

Some people start a business or a new venture and wonder why the breaks don't seem to come their way. They feel as though they're always swimming upstream. Why? It's because they haven't yet learned to believe in themselves. They are not applying the universal laws and principles that we've talked about throughout this book.

When we come to the end of our lives, I don't believe we're going to be haunted by our failures. I think we'll be haunted by our "what ifs."

What if I had gotten up one more time and gone after my goal? What if I hadn't quit so early on? What if I had done things that way? What if I had taken advantage of that opportunity that was laid right at my feet? The "what ifs" are killers, for sure. They're dream killers. Would you want your last thought on this Earth to be, "What if I had …?"

What is your goal? What is the dream that you've taken out of the closet, and dusted off, and chosen to pursue?

Another of my favorite movies is "City Slickers," with Billy Crystal. Maybe you remember this scene. Curly, played by the actor Jack Palance, tells Mitch, the Billy Crystal character, that the secret to life is just one thing. Curly holds up one finger and says, "One thing. Just one thing." When Mitch asks what the one thing is, Curly replies, "That's what you have to find out."

In my life, this has become my **one thing**: this crusade to make a difference in people's lives. It didn't happen instantly. There have been plenty of hardships and roadblocks along the way, but with every obstacle we've overcome, there have been more people who wanted to come along.

I've spent a lifetime looking for people and organizations where I can make a difference. You have to go find that one thing that is meant for you. You were meant to be here. The fact that you are reading this book is no accident; there's a message in this book that is just for you.

Once you find your one thing, there's nothing better. It's a wonderful, delicious feeling. You can focus all of your energies there, not only to make yourself better at that one thing, but also to share it with the world.

The people who quit too early may never find that one thing. Even sadder, they may find it but then walk away because it's too difficult.

That one thing is what the good Lord has put within you to make a difference in this world, in your world, and in the world around you. Don't ever be discouraged. There's a quote from Jeffrey R. Holland that sums it up: "Heaven is cheering for you today, tomorrow, and forever."

I firmly believe that. Why is Heaven cheering for you? Because Heaven knows that as you use that one thing, as you use that gift that you have, you're going to make this world a better place to be in. You're going to help a lot of people who are hurting. You're going to help people who are looking to find hope again in their lives. You're going to help them learn that miracles are possible.

Miracles happen

Do you remember the story of the Miracle on Ice? It happened in the 1980 Winter Olympics, in Lake Placid. In those days, the Soviet Union—the U.S.S.R.—had the best hockey team in the world. They were probably one of the best teams in the history of hockey. They had been together for years. Back then, professional athletes were not allowed to play in the Olympics, but Soviet athletes might as well have been professionals. They weren't really amateurs; all they did was play hockey. They didn't have to worry about a job or about supporting themselves because the Soviet Union took care of them.

The United States national team was made up of amateurs. They were mostly college-age, some just out of college. Their coach, Herb Brooks, told those young Americans from day one that they could beat the Soviets. He kept telling his players that beating the Soviets was not only possible but they were going to do it.

They worked hard to be as competitive as possible, but shortly before the Olympics opened, Team USA played the Soviet team in an exhibition match and got crushed. The Soviets just walked all over the U.S. team. It wasn't even a game.

The U.S players had a choice. They could have just rolled over and agreed with all the experts who said that the Soviet team was too strong for them. Instead, they all got back up off the ice, dusted themselves off, kept working hard, and continued to believe that their day was coming. When they finally met the Soviets in the Olympics, most of America was glued to the television set watching this epic match.

Herb Brooks fired up his players by telling them, "Great moments are born from great opportunity. You were born to be a player. You were meant to be here. This is your moment. This moment is yours. Now, go out there and take it."

Even if you're not old enough to remember it, you probably know what happened. To the shock of the entire sports world—and especially to the Soviet Union—Team USA beat the Soviet team and then went on to win the gold medal. It's one of the most inspirational stories I know.

If those young American kids could beat that accomplished Soviet team, what might you or I accomplish?

If one person can do it ...

Think of any of the examples I've offered throughout this book and imagine yourself in that situation. Another of our universal laws is this: If one person can do it, then it's available to all. People once believed it was humanly impossible to run a four-minute mile, but then Roger Bannister did it. And not long after he broke that barrier, once people had seen it was possible, other runners began to believe they could do it too, and so they did. Now a sub-four-minute mile is not unusual.

Remember, if one person does it, it's available to the rest of us. It just depends on how badly we want it, whatever it is, and how much work we are willing to put into it.

Ask yourself this: Today, right now, are you where you want to be? It's a simple question, but it demands an honest answer. Are you where you want to be in your love life, in your relationships, in your health, in your finances, in your education, in your job, in your career?

If your answer is no, then the next question is, are you willing to do something about it? Are you willing to work and get it? Belief and hard work together can accomplish miracles. What's the miracle you're looking for in your life?

Zig Ziglar, the great motivational speaker, used to tell a story about growing up poor in the South. His neighbors had a cook, Maude, who used to make biscuits every day. Ziglar said you could smell those biscuits all through the neighborhood, so he always tried to be around when Maude was making her biscuits. One day, when Maude pulled the biscuits out of the oven, they weren't the big fluffy type that he was used to seeing. They were all flat. He asked what had happened to them, and Maude said, "They squatted to rise, and they just got cooked in the squat." That's a great lesson for all of us. How often do we say that we're going to do something someday? We're going to get to it; we're going to make it happen, whatever it is. We squat to rise and then life gets in the way. Work gets in the way. Discouragement gets in the way. The realization that "this is harder than I thought" gets in the way and then we just get cooked in the squat. We never get to where we want. Don't let that happen to you or your dream.

Leading by example: Mac's story

You can't let yourself give up. I learned that lesson early from the person who has always been the biggest influence on me, my dad, Mac McLeod. He was a Marine in World War II, as was my uncle, Bud Neukam. They were both very proud members of the Marine Corps, and part of what Tom Brokaw has called "the greatest generation."

My dad was not only my favorite coach, but he was also my best friend. Throughout his life, my dad gave me examples of never giving up, of how to keep moving forward. When I would get down on myself, he was the one who would give me the pep talk to get me back up.

He led by example. He was never way behind the lines. He was always on the front line encouraging not just me but all of the ball players who ended up playing for him. Some of the championship teams that I was privileged to play on were coached by my dad.

He was a hard coach, but he was a fair coach. Everyone was treated the same. At the end of every game, whether we won or we lost, we would have a team meeting and he would give us his feedback. Because I was his son, he was usually harder on me than anyone else, which was fine with me. I expected that. In fact, one of my teammates from those days, Mike Smith, made me laugh when he told me not long ago that he stopped sitting next to me in those meetings because he finally realized that when my dad got done chewing on me, it would be the person next to me that he started on next. This is the same Mike Smith who actually played shortstop for us, in a championship game, with a broken shoulder.

I often say that my dad had the uncanny ability to attract ball players who were the poorest losers in the world. Every man on my dad's teams hated to lose with a passion. It was in their fiber and it was in their blood. I didn't know it then, but having learned since then about the reticular activating system, I can see that it was a perfect example of the RAS at work.

My dad didn't like second place. He did not like to lose. Therefore, winning was his inner picture. His RAS made sure his outside world was the same. We drew all players from all over the valley who wanted to play for my dad. We won many games and many championships.

My dad also taught every player who ever played for him that he could care less about what color your skin was, what nationality you were, what religion you practiced, or what language you spoke. The only thing that mattered to him was the color jersey that you were wearing. That was how I was raised, and all of his ballplayers learned the same.

My friend Don Anhder was also a recipient of my dad's coaching. Following his own dreams, Don later moved to a small farming community in Nevada to become a teacher and high school coach. There he led his teams to several state championships. He also became a leader in his church, serving and helping many people along the way. Don is still making a difference today.

I learned from my dad the importance of helping people. He was a champion of the underdog, always looking for folks who were down and out, or the person who just needed a break. After his coaching days, my dad served as national vice president of the American Federation of Government Employees (AFGE).

I remember my dad working tirelessly to help those people he represented. One example was a cafeteria worker at one of the big air bases. She had diabetes, serious enough that she had to have a snack or a bite to eat every couple of hours. She kept some cheese in her locker, and when she needed to eat, she would slip out to her locker, have a quick bite of cheese, and then hurry back to work.

One of the supervisors accused her of stealing her cheese from the cafeteria. They brought charges against her and fired her. After my dad talked to her and heard her side of the story, he went to bat for her. He defended her in a hearing at the air base.

No one ever expected the commander of the base to get involved in that kind of a hearing, but my dad somehow managed to compel the commander himself to testify.

To prepare for the hearing, my dad went to the grocery store and bought some cheese, the same kind of cheese that the cafeteria worker had brought to work to nibble on. He left it out for a few days so it would look like the supervisor's "evidence"—the piece of cheese that they had pulled out of the worker's locker in the locker room. By the time of the hearing, the piece of cheese that my dad bought at the grocery store looked just the same as the piece of cheese that they pulled out of the locker room. And since neither piece of cheese had been refrigerated for days, it really didn't look very good.

In the crowning moment of the entire hearing, my dad had the commander on the witness stand and challenged him to pick out which of the two pieces of cheese had been "stolen" from the cafeteria. Facing the possibility of guessing wrong, the commander backed down. Even though he had a 50/50 chance of guessing correctly, he didn't want to risk picking the wrong piece of cheese.

In the end, my dad was able to get the woman her job back. That was just one of the many, many examples that I saw of his helping individuals who had been left in a position where they couldn't help themselves. It was always an inspiration to our entire family, the legacy that he left behind in that union.

My dad also showed us what it means to never give up.

Every two years, he had to run for reelection to his position. One year, there was a power struggle within the local, with some things happening under the table. My dad wouldn't get down in the mud of that struggle and he lost the election. It was a bitter pill for him to swallow because he knew the person who replaced him couldn't do the job. But my dad didn't come home with his tail between his legs. He came home holding his head high, because in his heart he knew that in the previous two years he had done the best he could do for the people. He didn't quit. He didn't roll over and play dead. He went back to work helping people, and he also prepared himself for the next election two years later. There was no "woe is me"; there were no pity parties.

Knowing how much my dad really did not like to lose, I saw in him a marvelous example of picking yourself up and getting back in the game of life. Sure enough, two years later he won back his position in a landslide because the people had had enough of his successor. From then on my dad won every AFGE election until his retirement. When he retired, he personally picked his successor, a woman named

Andrea Brooks. He endorsed her to win his position, and she won the next election, in large part because my dad was on her team. She ended up doing a great job.

He was remembered at AFGE for years. Several years after my dad passed away, the union had a convention at the Tropicana Hotel here in Las Vegas. I was really missing my dad at the time, so I went out to the meeting site. I went to the registration table and explained that I didn't have credentials for the meeting but was hoping to just take a look, because of my dad's previous work as national vice president of the union.

One of the gentlemen who was checking in overheard my story and asked, "Are you talking about Mac McLeod?" I said, "Yes, sir. That's my dad." He spent the next 10 minutes telling me what a great dad I had, and how many people he had helped, and what a great example he was to the everyday, common working man. I was overwhelmed. As I walked back to my car, I was literally fighting tears because it was such a proud moment. That's the legacy that my dad left behind.

What is the legacy you and I are going to leave behind? It is a choice. It's our choice. It's **your** choice.

14. The Magic Wand

People who wait for a magic wand
fail to see that they ARE the magic wand.
Thomas Leonard

In every training I do, and with every student I mentor, I always ask this question: If I had a magic wand that I could wave over you and you would have the life you've always dreamed of, what would that look like?

Now, I'm certainly not the first person to ask this question. Psychologists use it as a tool; you can find plenty of research on it. What I like about this question though, is that it opens up possibilities that don't come up any other way.

Sometimes I even bring a magic wand with me to my talks, and I can tell you that everyone there wants that wand waved over them. There's something about the idea of a magic wand that takes us back to childhood. For me it brings back memories of when I was a kid and everything seemed possible. It's like walking through the gates of Disneyland, as we talked about in a previous chapter.

Guess what? You have your own magic wand within you. It's in your brain; it's on that belief window that we've been talking about. It's in the principles we've been discussing throughout this book. They're the building blocks of your magic wand:

Examine your beliefs.

Abandon your escape route.

Leave no doubt.

Surround yourself with positive input.

Reframe your negative self-talk.

Invest in yourself.

Claim your gifts.

See yourself for who you really are.

Choose your road.

Never give up.

See, you do have a magic wand! Don't ever let anyone tell you that you don't. Each of us has this magic wand, and you can use it to follow your dream. You can wave it over yourself, and you can wave it over other people to help them start believing in their own dream too.

It's time to dust off those dreams that you've had in the past. Maybe you've stuck them in the closet; maybe they're covered in cobwebs and dust. It's time to go revisit them. Pull them out, dust them off, and take a look at them through your new belief window. Remember, we discarded all those old beliefs that don't serve us any longer. Now it's time to believe in that dream, because now you have the tools to make it happen. Now you've got that magic wand. But you have to use it!

I know that you could just read this book for entertainment and then set it aside with other stuff to gather dust. Don't let that happen. Learn from what we've discussed here. Take these principles and put them into action.

By now you know that none of this is theory. All of these principles and tools have been field-tested. I know that they work because I've used them myself and I've watched hundreds of other people use them. There's a saying, "It works if you work it." That's so true. In this book, I've offered many stories and many strategies. Pick out the ones that you like and put them to use. You will see that they make a difference in your life.

You may wonder why I'm so passionate about sharing what I've learned with you. There's a quote—yes, another quote!—that I have lived by for years. It was said by Mary Augusta Ward: "Every man is bound to leave a story better than he found it." I firmly believe that, and I've made it a guiding principle for my daily life.

Every person has a story, and I believe that when I meet that person, it's up to me to make that story better, even if it's just for a moment. I believe we all owe it to each other to do that. It doesn't matter whether you are talking to a stranger, or a friend, or a family member. Make sure that you leave them feeling better about themselves than when you found them. That goes for the hostess who seats you at the restaurant. That goes for the server who waits on you. That goes for the clerk in the grocery store or that sales person in the shopping mall. That goes for anyone who comes across your path. It's part of waving your magic wand over them.

My wife will tell you that wherever we go, I am always starting conversations with people, and I always make sure to give them a sincere compliment. You can't be phony about it; people will see right through that. But you can always find a reason to compliment them. It might be, "Wow, you have a great smile," or "Wow, I love your energy," or "Wow, I love the service you have given me and my wife today." People do not get enough compliments. I think it's a lost art.

Have you ever noticed, when you give someone a compliment, all of a sudden they just light up? I've seen it time and again. They light up just like a Christmas tree. Isn't that wonderful that we can do that? Is it a lot of work? No. It's just being a human being and complimenting another human being.

That's part of my own crusade: bringing back those simple acts of kindness. It's about being an uplifting influence. It's all about taking a little woe off someone's back and leaving people better off than we found them.

When you help people learn to feel better about their lives and to believe in themselves, the possibilities are endless.

I once took over a baseball team that really was not very good. For two whole years, they had won very few games. As soon as I got there I knew we had to change the team's mental outlook. We had to change what was on their collective belief window. So we went to work. We worked all through the summer, playing games and having many practices. After every practice we would have a meeting, and I would do visualization with them. I would tell them what we were going to end up accomplishing.

When I first started talking to them about winning championships, I'm sure most of them thought I was blowing smoke. But there was not a doubt in any of their minds that I believed in what I was saying. My task was to get them to believe it, and eventually they did start to believe. And we started to win.

That very first year we went on to beat a team that had beaten us pretty badly during the season. There were a lot of older kids on that team and my players were much younger. But we faced them in the championship game and won the game. It was wonderful to see. Any time I coached kids or mentored kids, all I wanted for them was to have that one moment of victory in life—that defining moment when they know they are the best of the best.

There's nothing better for your self-esteem; that kind of experience can last a lifetime. When we won that first year, a lot of people thought we must have gotten lucky. Luck had nothing to do with it. We won because we outworked everybody and we out-believed everybody. The next year we reached the championship game again. We were facing the same team we had beaten the year before, so they were definitely carrying a grudge against us. But we won again, because again, we outworked and out-believed our opponents.

Now here in Las Vegas, it gets very hot in the summer sun. Games are normally played at night, under the lights, when it's a little cooler. But our team practiced every Saturday in the heat. When we first starting doing that, in my first year with the team, the players complained about having to practice in the heat of the day. I would tell them, "One day we're going to be in a tournament and have to play in the heat. When that day comes, we are going to be used to it and the teams we are playing are going to wilt from the heat."

The complaints stopped after we won the championship that first year. In the third year, we were in the tournament again, chasing our third straight championship, when the Friday night games got rained out. Sure enough, that meant we would have to play day games on Saturday, in the middle of July in Las Vegas. Even I was surprised by how excited my team was. They knew that for three years we'd practiced in the heat for this one moment. They were ready and they knew the other teams wouldn't be.

Was that what made the difference? I can't tell you for sure that it did but I do know this: It absolutely made a difference in the belief pattern of my players. They knew they were ready. Sure enough, we won both of those day games and with them another championship.

That team became a dynasty. We won five years in a row, and in most of those years, we beat teams who were better than we were. How? By now, you know my answer: hard work and belief always pay off.

What did that experience do for those kids? They had been getting beaten over and over again. They didn't have much self-esteem left. They started winning, and eventually each of them was able to have that defining moment of knowing they were the best of the best.

I used to tell my players, "When it comes to the championship, I don't care if the trophy is no bigger than a dime. What really matters is that you know that for this one moment in time, you're the best." Every one of those kids went on to success in their lives. Cindy and I ran into one of them at a meeting a while back. His name is Ronnie York, and he had been my center fielder. He told my wife, "Barry McLeod was the toughest coach I ever played for," but he said it with great pride because he was part of those championship teams. Today Ronnie is a success in the banking industry, and still making a difference out there for those around him.

There are many stories like that about a lot of the other players and the successes they've had. I will always be grateful for my small part in building their self-esteem and self-confidence. They learned that nothing is impossible if you believe. As it says in the scriptures, "All things are possible to those who believe" (Mark 9:23). I have seen the evidence time and time again throughout my life.

There's a line in the movie "Field of Dreams" that I love. Of course the line most people remember from that movie is "if you build it, they will come." My favorite is a different line from that same scene. James Earl Jones' character,

Terence, is urging Ray, played by Kevin Costner, not to give up or sell his farm. He assures him that it's going to happen—that people will come to his baseball field. He tells Ray, "It will be as if they dipped themselves in magic waters." I love that line because I know that is what's possible for each of us.

Once you join a crusade such as the one we are talking about in this book—to make a difference in people's lives, your own and others'—it gets inside of you. The mission gets into your blood; it gets into your belief window; it gets into your RAS. It really is as if we've been dipped in magic waters—or touched by a magic wand—because everything changes. You become that maniac on a mission, and nothing is impossible to you. It's wonderful. You deserve to have that.

Guy Kawasaki, who is one of the most successful entrepreneurs of our time, describes himself as a secular evangelist. He argues that personal success depends on believing in yourself and your goal or cause with the passion of an evangelist. In his book *Selling the Dream,* he says, "To the luckiest of people, a time comes when they join or launch a cause that forever changes their lives and the lives of others. Losing yourself in a cause is delicious and intoxicating. The best word to describe the sensation is 'crusade.'"

I believe that each of us was born with a crusade within us. That life you've always wanted is possible. Go find your crusade and run with it. I'm cheering for you.

Conclusion

Thank you for taking the time to read *The Book of Barry*. Although I've been living and teaching these principles for many years, putting them to paper was a big decision for me. It would not have happened without my wife's encouragement and the support of so many others who have urged me to write it.

As I said in the introduction, my mission is to make the world a better place by making a difference in people's lives. This book is part of that mission, and if this book makes a difference in just one person's life then we will have accomplished what we set out to do.

I want to leave you, the reader, with a challenge to join me on this crusade to make a difference out in the world. There are so many hurting people and so many tough situations all around us. Just a word of hope can make a lasting difference in someone's life.

This is a crusade. I just want people to realize that each of us individually has the power to change the world: to make a difference in people's lives, to pick each other up, to dust each other off, and to move forward again one more time.

Join these crusaders who have already joined us. Take what you've learned in this book and apply it. Whatever gift you have, let's sharpen it. Use it every day. Look again at the stories we've told here. These are all stories of real people. Learn from them and put those lessons to use.

Believe fearlessly in your cause. Believe with all of your heart, body, and soul. Let it get into your blood and stir your deepest passion. Think of all the hurting people who need to have hope brought back into their lives. We can do that. You and I have that message of hope. If you want to be a hope crusader and join us, then it's time to take action. It's time to do something about it. Take back control of your life and destiny, not only for yourself, but for your family and all the other families out there.

It's a noble cause. It should give you goosebumps. Come join us. Let's go out there and make a difference together. **I believe in you**.

Suggestions for Further Reading

Here are just a few of my favorite books for you to consider:

As a Man Thinketh by James Allen

Brass Tacks: The Essentials of Permanent Success by Richard Burnett

How to Use the Laws of Mind by Joseph Murphy

Jonathan Livingston Seagull by Richard Bach

The Bible, King James Version

The Book of Mormon

The Energy Bus by John Gordon

Who Are You Really and What Do You Want? by Shad Helmstetter

Think and Grow Rich by Napoleon Hill

The Greatest Salesman in the World by Og Mandino

3 Things Successful People Do: The Road Map That Will Change Your Life by John C. Maxwell

The Magic of Thinking Big by David J. Schwartz

The Power of Perception by Hyrum W. Smith

The Success System that Never Fails by Clement W. Stone

Gratitude

With enormous gratitude to those who have taught me lessons in life, love, and business:

Don Anhder

George and Dr. Donna Antarr

Sam and Vi Aston

Ray Atkin

Cindy Benner

Scott V. Black

Jeff and Angela Boyle

David and Angie Buckles

Kirby and Shirley Burgess

Richard Burnett

Lori Davis

Steven Goldstein

Stan Haley

Roxanne James

Jake Jenson

Richard and Brenda Johnson

Captain Michael Johnston

Rick Karstedt

Mike and Joann Knapp

Pat and Tonio Kohl

Dennis and Maureen Muaina

David Nelson

Les Perryman

Jacki Smith

Mike Smith

Dan Souza

John and Sharon Williams

Eric Yugar

I would also like to thank my editor, Judith Jones, and my publisher, Michael DeLon, for all their help in making *The Book of Barry* a reality.

About Barry

Barry McLeod is a coach, a trainer, and a 30-year network marketing specialist. His experience comes from his education by great leaders such as W. Clement Stone's *The Success System That Never Fails*, where he earned National Honors Recognition for selling 100 policies in a week. He also trained agents in the art of selling seminars for Richard Burnett's *Top Gun Training*. As recruiting and training director for Family Heritage Insurance and Blue Cross Blue Shield, Barry developed training programs in the art of cold-calling and door-to-door sales. He is a Master Graduate of Rapport Leadership International, in Las Vegas, Nevada, where he completed courses in Leadership I, Leadership II, Fire Walk, Power Communications, and Wealth Mastery.

Barry, as a sports enthusiast, brings his experience and passion for coaching ball-teams into training and motivating others to believe in themselves. He had the privilege of coaching or playing on 17 different championship teams, which inspired him to recognize the power of belief. His goal is to aggressively build large organizations of passionate crusaders. The driving forces in Barry's life are the lessons learned from his late father, his favorite coach and very best friend.

Barry currently resides in Las Vegas, Nevada, with his wife Cindy, their seven children, twelve grandchildren, and three dogs.

Barry with two of his students

Sources

A–Z Quotes. http://www.azquotes.com/author/
4000-Walt_Disney.

———. http://www.azquotes.com/author/4000-
Walt_Disney?p=2.

———. http://www.azquotes.com/author/4358-
Thomas_A_Edison.

———. http://www.azquotes.com/author/7843-
Helen_Keller?p=10.

———. http://www.azquotes.com/author/8733-
Thomas_Leonard.

———. http://www.azquotes.com/author/8044-
Martin_Luther_King_Jr.

———. http://www.azquotes.com/author/
10824-Earl_Nightingale?p=2.

———. http://www.azquotes.com/author/
15079-Queen_Victoria.

Acres of Diamonds. http://www.nightingale.com/
articles/acres-of-diamonds.

Bateman, Kody. MLM Blueprint: Your Subconscious
Journey to Network Marketing Success. Salt Lake City:
Eagle One Publishing, 2012.

Choisin Reservoir. http://www.chosinreservoir
.com/.

Churchill Centre, The. http://www.winston
churchill.org/the-life-of-churchill/life.

———. http://www.winstonchurchill.org
/publications/finest-hour/finest-hour-136/media-
matters.

"Cortés, Hernán." International Encyclopedia of the Social
Sciences. 2008. Encyclopedia.com.
http://www.encyclopedia.com/doc/1G2-
3045300468.html

Covey, Steven. *The 7 Habits of Highly Effective People.* New
York: Free Press, 1990.

Dyer, Wayne W. Real Magic: Creating Miracles in Everyday
Life. HarperCollins, 1992.

Encyclopedia Britannica. https://www.britannica
.com/event/Battle-of-Britain-European-history-1940.

———. https://www.britannica.com/event
/Battle-of-the-Chosin-Reservoir.

Helmstetter, Shad. *What to Say When You Talk to Yourself.*
New York: Pocket Books, 1990.

History.com. http://www.history.com
/topics/world-war-ii/battle-of-britain

Kawasaki, Guy. *Selling the Dream*. New York: HarperBusiness, 1992.

Keyes, Ken, Jr. *The Hundredth Monkey*. Vision Books, 1982.

Les Brown Official Site. http://www.lesbrown .com/about-les/quotes.html.

Marine Corps Association & Foundation. https:// www.mca-marines.org/leatherneck/marine-corps-quotes#.

Military Quotes. http://www.military-quotes.com/churchill.htm.

National Baseball Hall of Fame. http:// baseballhall.org/hof/paige-satchel.

New York Times, The. http://www.nytimes.com /2002/09/05/business/clement-stone-dies-at-100-built-empire-on-optimism.html.

Satchel Paige—The Official Website. http:// www.satchelpaige.com/.

———. http://www.satchelpaige.com/bio2.html.

———. http://www.satchelpaige.com/quote2 .html.

Stone, W. Clement. *The Success System That Never Fails*. Prentice Hall, 1962.

Temple University. https://www.temple.edu
/about/history/acres-diamonds.

W. Clement & Jessie V. Stone Foundation. http://
www.wcstonefnd.org/history.

The Book of Barry
Sage Advice for Life, Love, and Business

Barry & Cindy McLeod
1113 Silvery Shadow Ave
Henderson, NV 89015

Barry: debtfree2@cox.net
Cindy: thinkwinwin@ymail.com

www.TheBookOfBarry.com

ISBN-13: 978-0-9883878-9-8
ISBN-10: 0-9883878-9-1

—Disclaimer—

Although the author and publisher have made every effort to ensure that the information in this book was correct at press time, the author and publisher do not assume and hereby disclaim any liability to any party for any loss, damage, or disruption caused by errors or omissions, whether such errors or omissions result from negligence, accident, or any other cause.

www.ExpertPress.net

www.ingramcontent.com/pod-product-compliance
Lightning Source LLC
Chambersburg PA
CBHW052052090426
42739CB00010B/2143